'A LIFE DIVIDED''

Ms Helen Bethea

ISBN: 1453636277
ISBN-13: 9781453636275
Library of Congress Control Number: 2010908999

TABLE OF CONTENTS

THE BIRTH CERTIFICATES

Looking forward to going to Cancun, Mexico, in the month of January was exciting. You see, my son was getting married. He and his beautiful bride-to-be decided to have their wedding in Cancun, on the beach in a beautiful gazebo that was decorated with colorful balloons, flowers, and sheer fabrics that flowed in the breeze coming off the ocean. This was a breathtaking scene, with family and friends partaking in the exchange of marriage vows between two special young people.

Well, in the midst of preparing for this exciting trip, we (my daughter and I) thought we had to have passports; therefore, we went online (you can do almost everything online these days) and pulled up the application to apply for a passport.

We knew we needed birth certificates, and I knew that was not a problem because I had mine. After filling out the application, I printed it out, and then I gathered my papers and went to the main post office to apply for my passport. I was sitting in the waiting room for maybe an hour—I was early, and the office was closed for lunch—looking around and wondering if I was the only one applying for a passport. Finally, this gentleman walked into the waiting area, and I wondered if he was the one to open the office. Sure enough, he was. I was getting anxious. After he opened the office and started helping the other customers, it was my turn. I went into the office and gave the man my application; he looked it over and asked, "Do you have your birth certificate?"

"Oh yes, I do." I gave him my birth certificate, the one I had for over forty years. I was excited and smiling, knowing this was going to happen; I was getting my passport. Well, the man burst my bubble!

He looked at me and said, "This is not a valid birth certificate." My mouth flew open, and probably all the flies, if there were any in there, visited my tonsils!

My first thought was, *Oh no, this can't be happening again.* After collecting myself, I asked him "Why isn't it valid?"

In a pleasant, calm voice he answered, "Well, there is no state seal stamped on it."

Okay! Now, what do I do? I picked up my papers, with my head down, and literally dragged myself out of the office, in a daze, and then out of the building and into the car. I sat there for a few minutes, holding back the tears and feeling so alone. I reminded myself, "I am not a young woman anymore—not that I'm an old one either—but, how many times will I have to wonder who I am and who I belong to?"

This is the same birth certificate that was given to me by my adopted mother in 1962. It was my adopted mother who replaced the original birth certificate that she altered when she tried to cover up my race.

As I drove home, all kind of thoughts went through my mind. In my mind, I asked my adopted mother, *Why did you tamper with my birth certificate, why couldn't you leave things alone?* I knew she couldn't answer me—and hoped she wouldn't answer me, if you know what I mean.

Once I got home, I calmed down and called my daughter. "Guess what," I said. "I couldn't get my passport!" When she asked what had happened, I was still upset, so I told her that grown people have a way of messing up your life, and that I had a birth certificate that wasn't valid.

She said to me, "Mom, call the Bureau of Vital Statistics in South Carolina and tell them you need a copy of your birth certificate."

"Okay," I responded. "I will, thanks, and I love you. I'll let you know what happens."

I called the Bureau of Vital Statistics in South Carolina. When a woman answered, I told her my name and that I needed a copy of my birth certificate. She replied with questions such as "what is your date of birth? What is your mothers' maiden name? What is your place of birth?"

After I gave her the information, she put me on hold. It only took her a few minutes, maybe five or so, and then she said to me, "Ma'am, I have a folder here with the name of the person you gave me, but you are not listed as one of her siblings." She then started to name my siblings."

This was music to my ears; I heard her reading off the names of my siblings, my brothers and my sister. I almost yelled in the phone—I may have—but I stopped her and said, "That's my family, you found it!"

She then said (and here's the kicker), "But your name is not there." When I asked her why it was not, she answered, "Because you were adopted in 1963, your name was removed from that family. Therefore, you are not legally part of that family, anymore."

I wanted to reach through the phone and grab that woman and do a Gary Coleman on her. "What ya talking about? Why are you telling me this stuff?" *Okay,* I told myself, *stay calm.* She said, "You are no longer on record as that person." I said to her, "You mean to tell me, because I was adopted, I have been permanently removed from my birth mothers records?" *How, unfair!*

She asked me for my adopted name, and I wanted tell her, *"You have all the answers, why ask me?"* But I didn't; I gave her my adopted name. She put me on hold to listen to that ridiculous music again. She came back and said, "I have a birth certificate for you under your adopted name."

"Thank you! Send me two copies please." I wasn't satisfied with what I had learned and intended to try and understand what and why this had happened.

I later decided to call my sister to share this information with her. I told her what I had learned from the lady at the Bureau of Vital Statistics.

My sister told me, "Don't worry, mama decided a few years ago to get birth certificates of all the children. I'll look in a purse she kept all the documents in, and I'll call you back." I was excited and could hardly wait for her to return my call. When she called me, and she said, "I went through mama's purse and found all the birth certificates; yours is there." This meant my original birth certificate; no more false information. She told me that she would put my birth certificate in the mail to me. A few days later, I received the birth certificate from my sister, the one my mama had gotten in 1973, with information about my birth. Now, I have two birth certificates, one with my adopted parents and one with my birth parents.

What I don't understand is how being adopted can cause one to loose her biological identity, the one that she is born with. It's as if that person doesn't exist anymore. Following the incident with my birth certificate, I requested a copy of my adoption papers from the courthouse in South Carolina. It wasn't hard to do—because of my age at the time of the adoption, my records were not sealed, therefore, I was able to get a copy. The only thing that confused me was the date: the representative from the Bureau of Vital Statistics said I was adopted in 1963; my adoption papers stated the year to be 1950. There seems to be conflicting information from somewhere.

The thing is, I was old enough to know who my family was and where they were. I knew that I was adopted; therefore, my true identify was not hidden from me. There are so many people out there who have been adopted and don't have a clue to the truth about their birth parents. If your adopted or biological parents don't tell you the truth, believe me, someone else will.

Why risk being twenty years or older and learning that the family you thought was yours turns out not to be your biological parents? What if you get sick or have an illness, and they might need a kidney or bone marrow or blood, and learn that you are not a match with the adopted parents? The adopted parents don't want to say anything because the truth would have to be told. This could be a life-threatening situation for the adopted person. Or, you could meet someone fall in love and want to get married—only to find out that you are related to that person. All kinds of situations can come about when you don't know your family history. I know sometimes circumstances can prevent someone from knowing who her biological parents are and, perhaps there is a reason that she shouldn't know, but that should be carefully thought out. A child should have the right to know the truth.

We need to be told by those who love and care for us. It is better than going to a family reunion or funeral, or running into Ms. Suzie Mae, who can't wait to tell you what she knows about you and your family. She will tell everything and some. There are people who can't handle Ms. Suzie Mae's words: "Girl, I know when they brought you here! You know that ain't your real momma and daddy?" If you already know the truth, though, then she's the one who looks like an idiot. However, why take that chance with someone else's life?

The adopted person will probably love you even more for being honest with them. Let her decide if she wants to have a relationship with her biological parents or parent; it should be her decision. There are grandparents, aunts, uncles—a whole family out there who would be ecstatic to know that that person is part of them.

I have gotten completely off track from where I should be, because I was talking about my birth certificate and my son's wedding. We didn't need the passports after all, but we went to Cancun and had a ball.

MY LIFE WITH MY BIOLOGICAL FAMILY

When I was born in 1943, my mama held me in her arms in the bedroom at our house. My sister always wanted to rub my tummy and brush my hair because it was curly, and she called me her baby doll.

Daddy told her, "This is your little baby sister; she is not a baby doll, so be careful." My sister was the eldest, and I had a brother who was the next oldest. Then, a few years later, after I was born, my mama had another son, our younger brother. We lived in a four- or five-room, wood-framed house in the rural part of South Carolina.

We spent a lot of time at our grandma's house, which was large with a kitchen that was attached to the back of the house by a long, wooden porch. In this kitchen, I will always remember the round table with a lazy Susan in the middle. That table held the best country food for us to eat—fried chicken, fresh vegetables, rice, and gravy. A black lady—I don't remember her name—was the one who cooked for my grandma. There were other black people on my grandma's place who helped run the saw mill and worked the tobacco fields, along with the other crops that she grew.

My cousins, brothers, and other children played in the yard at my grandma's house. We played in the woods, jumping ditches and playing in the sawdust at the saw mill. There was something about playing in the sawdust—it was cool, and it seemed to get the dirt off of our feet.

My grandma offered a service to many people from North and South Carolina. She performed services that helped with the mind and body, as well as their soul-searching problems. She told them things by looking at their palms. Whatever she did helped her clients understand their life situations. She prepared potions from different kinds of herbs and gave it to them.

My father became ill and passed away at a young age. This left my mama with four children to raise and care for. She took care of us by sewing for other people. We always ate at grandma's house. Therefore, she didn't have to worry about feeding us.

My oldest brother and sister went to school everyday, and my younger brother and I spent our time at grandmas. Since I was older than my younger brother, I should have been in school with my other siblings, but I wasn't. I remember the one time I went to school with my sister and brother, and that was the last time I went with them. The people at the school said I looked too much like a black child with my curly hair, and I guess my skin tone was a little browner. I couldn't go to the black school because they knew my family was white. So there you go; I wasn't in school. So, Social Services decided to visit my mama, threatening to put me in an orphanage. If my sister knew the Social Service Agents were there or coming she would take me and hide in the cornfield so they couldn't find me.

LIVING WITH MY STEPFATHER AND MAMA

My mama met and married my stepfather, who drove a pulp truck. When my stepfather wasn't driving his truck, he was drinking. He drank a lot and was always cussing.

At an early age, maybe five, I was in the living room at my mama's house. My stepfather was in the room, and he was standing over me holding his penis in his hand. He said, "Here gal, put this in your mouth!" I don't know if I did or not; I guess I blocked it out of my mind. There were times when I would think about that incident, but I never said anything to anyone about it. Two years ago, I asked my sister about what my stepfather did, asking if it did happen, or if I imagined it.

She said, "Lord, I was hoping you would never remember that!" I told her I did and she said well nothing happened, and she asked me if I remembered who stopped him. I told her, "No!" She said. "Well, I did, and I told him I would kill him if he every touched you again." She told mama what my stepfather had done to me. My mama told him, "Don't you ever put your hands on her again!"

He didn't bother me again. I remember coming back to visit after becoming an adult, my stepfather was sitting on the sofa next to Mama and as usual he was cussing and Mama said to him, "Stop cussing around her; she isn't used to hearing that kind of talk."

I told mama, "That's okay; I have heard that kind of talk before."

My stepfather looked at me and said, "Girl, don't you know I will whip your a--!"

I said back to him, "What do you think I will be doing while you are doing that?"

He looked at me in amazement, because I had never spoken up to him before. He started crying and said to me, "I'm sorry for the way I treated you; I'm sorry." I did not say anything, he just looked so small, this giant of a man that tried to sexually molest me when I was just a little girl. He died a few years later; he choked to death on a piece of beef that he was eating for dinner.

Mama had three rooms in the house we lived in. She had two full size beds in one of the large rooms for us kids to sleep in. My two brothers slept in one and my sister and I slept in the other one. After a year or so, Mama gave birth to two more children that were boys, and they too shared that room with us. She would put quilts on the floor and made pallets for them to sleep on.

Some mornings for breakfast, Mama gave us corn flakes with milk, and we also ate sandwiches that we made with white sliced bread, butter, and sugar. We drank coffee that was sweetened with molasses because sometimes we didn't have sugar. Mama made wonderful jelly rolls for us kids to eat that were the best in the world. We had an icebox that had a block of ice placed in the bottom compartment that would keep leftover food and milk from spoiling.

People bought flour that was used to make bread and to cook with; it was always in big cloth sacks. These sacks had pretty printed flowers on them, that Mama washed and made dresses for my sister and me to wear.

Grandma needed certain kinds of roots that she used in her business to help her clients. She told us kids what to look for and where to look in the woods for the roots that she needed. When we found what she wanted we brought them to her and sometimes she gave us money in exchange for the roots.

When it was getting dark it was time to go home to Mama's house, which was about a half mile down the road from Grandma's house. We would ride on the back of the stripped-down truck that belonged to my stepfather or we had to walk alongside the highway in the dark and sometimes it was cold. A stripped-down truck is one that has no bed on the back; there is just the frame of a trailer.

We didn't have running water, so we had to use a pump for drinking water and to take a bath. Unfortunately, Mama's pump wasn't working; therefore, we had to get water from an aunt's house; the house seemed to be on a hill when I was a little girl. We had buckets that we used to fetch the water in. Because the buckets were heavy coming back filled with water, we spilled most of it, but we had enough to drink and to use it for whatever mama needed. I learned a few years ago that the house we went to for water belonged to our daddy's sister.

I remember my mama grew asparagus and strawberries in the backyard, and she had a goat that supplied milk for us. I learned later that I had to drink goat's milk as a baby because I had problems digesting the regular milk.

One Christmas when I was a little girl, we were all in bed. As I lay there waiting for Santa Claus to come, my sister would tell us to be good and that we better go to sleep. Well, I did not know until 2007, that the soft furry hand that went across my face on Christmas Eve was not Santa Claus it was my sister's hand with a furry glove on it. We believed everything she told us.

I remember my mama sent me to live with a family that lived somewhere in North Carolina. They did not have any children. I remember going to school in a one-room building, with a wood—burning, pot-bellied stove to keep us warm. There was not a whole lot to remember about that brief time, except one little boy whose name was Redelle. I don't know why he had such an impact in my memory; maybe because he had such an unusual name.

I had chores to do after school, and I specifically remember one of those chores was sitting in the backyard, churning butter. I had a bedroom to myself, and they were really nice people.

Grandma's husband could have been related to this family, because they looked as though they were Native American Indian. I didn't stay with them very long because I went back to live with my family. My grandma's husband, my step-grandfather, had the characteristics of a Native American Indian, but I can't truthfully say he was. He came from North Carolina and I thought he knew the family I lived with for a short while. I was sent there so I could go to school; perhaps my mother and grandmother thought I would fit in with that family and the people that lived there. I don't remember how long I stayed or why I was sent back to live with my family.

LIVING WITH
MY ADOPTED FAMILY

Lennie, the woman from Dillon who often asked my grandma whose child I was, came back to see her one day. This time, she must have talked with my grandma and my mama, because they told me "We are going to let you go home with this nice woman; she will take care of you and send you to school, so you be good and listen to her."

I thought I was going for a visit and that I would be back, like when I went to visit the other family. I wasn't happy about leaving, but what choice did I have? I was a little kid and had to do as I was told. My sister couldn't hide me in the cornfield anymore; this was different, and I was moving away from my family, my mama, brothers, and my sister and from the life that I was used to.

I said my goodbyes, crying and hoping that someone would say, "You don't have to go!" But that didn't happen. I was put in the car and rode away; we rode up the hill on the dirt road from grandma's house and onto the main road to Dillon.

When we arrived in Dillon, which seemed like a very long ride, we stopped in front of this building that had two stories. Lennie took me inside the building that had a juke box; I saw lots of candy and chips that were on shelves against the wall, and there were sodas and beer. There were booths and a place where people could sit on stools and eat, I guess. This was a restaurant, and I would be staying with her and her family.

She showed me the kitchen and introduced me to some women who were in the place, including her mother. Lennie was a short woman that was brown-skinned a little chunky, with pretty, long black, straight hair that she wore in a bun on top of her head. She wore glasses, and she dressed very nice. Her mother was similar in stature, only she seemed taller than Lennie and her hair was gray in color and kind of wavy; she, too, wore her hair in a bun at the back of her head.

Lennie's husband was there also; he was short like her and darker-skinned than she was, small in stature and seemed to be a nice man. When she introduced them to me, she told me to call her and her husband by their first names and to call her mother, Mother Emma.

Then she showed me where I would be sleeping. We went into a small hallway, which had a lot of steps that led to rooms that were on another floor. She said, "This is where you will sleep." I was going to share the same room with her mother. There was one full-size bed, a table, and a table with a mirror on it. There were three more bedrooms up there; one was hers and her husband's. There was another room that she used to store clothes and other stuff in.

After showing me where I would be living, she took me down-stairs and showed me the kitchen and a dining room. There was a backyard that had a dog, and there were chickens running around. There was a storage building and a smokehouse where she stored meat. In the very back, behind the storage building, was the outhouse. Now, I don't have to tell you what that is.

She told me that if I wanted something to eat, to tell her, her husband, or her mother. I saw all that candy and those cookies and knew I would have a good time eating that stuff. I would be able to drink a Pepsi all by myself; before, I always had to share with my brothers. I had never seen anything like this before.

Mother Emma was funny; she told me stories that made me laugh. She always dipped snuff; she carried a small tin can with a lid to keep it closed in her dress or apron pocket. The snuff she used was called Railroad Mill, and it was cased in a red bladder that was made out of some kind of plastic-looking stuff.

After getting settled, Lennie told me that Saturday night was bath night. There was a tin tub that was upstairs in the room I shared with Mother Emma. Lennie bought a lot of clothes for me, such as dresses, socks, and shoes for me to wear to church and school. The shoes for church were black patent leather.

On a Friday night after arriving there, Lennie told me she was going to wash my hair, which she did. Because I had long, thick hair, it took her awhile to get it dry, and then, for the first time, I experienced a hot comb. Lennie sat me down on a short stool between her legs and started combing my hair; she parted it and put some kind of grease on my scalp and the hair. Then, she laid this black comb that had a wooded handle on one end and a black, iron-looking comb on the other end, on a hot stove. When the comb got hot, she started using it to comb through my hair; I could hear a sizzling sound and assumed this was the grease touching the comb.

I had never had this done to my hair before, so I wasn't sure what was going on. I just know she pushed my head down and continued to use this comb on my hair. She told me to be still, or I would get burned. I learned later that she was straightening my hair with a hot comb and used grease to help keep the hair straight and so it wouldn't be so dry. I remember my mama using a lilt perm on my hair, but that was not what Lennie was doing. This process seemed like it took forever, because I had to sit still, and my little butt was tired. She parted my hair down the middle and put it in two pony-tails, which she braided and tied with colorful ribbons. Then, she put barrettes on the ends to keep the braid from coming loose.

On Saturday's, Lennie had a lot of people inside the joint or restaurant. I had never heard the kind of music that was played in the joint before; it was blues and rock and roll. I was used to hear-ing country music. I had seen people drunk and cussing before, because they did that back in Society Hill where I was from.

The people were in the joint until after midnight; there was a lot of loud talking and dancing going on downstairs. The music was so loud, you could feel the beat throughout the building. The noise was almost as bad as the trains when they came through Dillon. (We lived beside the railroad tracks.)

Lennie and her husband sold corn liquor for fifty cents a shot, and sometimes, they sold the liquor in half-pint bottles. Mother Emma was often upstairs, pouring this stuff into half-pint bottles from gallon mason jars by using a funnel. This was their way of mak-ing extra money. (They were Bootlegging moonshine.) Of course, this was illegal, but as long as you didn't get caught, who cared?

There was a black police officer in Dillon; he was a tall, slim man and was very nice and well respected. I am sure he knew what was going on at Lennie's and her husband's joint—the fact that they were selling moonshine—but I guess he did not say anything. However, someone turned them in because the police came and raided the restaurant. The police came upstairs, looked everywhere trying to find the liquor; they found some that they confiscated, and then they arrested her husband. He had to spend Saturday night in jail and was released and returned home on Sunday morning in time for church.

On Sundays, you had to go to church, no matter what. Lennie had me dressed in one of those pretty store-bought dresses for church. She put ribbons in my hair, and I wore my new shiny, black patent-leather shoes for church. I had never been to church before, so I did not know what to expect.

Lennie always cooked breakfast, which was hot grits cooked with plenty of homemade butter; there was sausage, bacon, or country ham (the kind that was cured in the smokehouse), fresh hen eggs, and homemade biscuits with homemade jelly or preserves.

As you can see, I ate well, and the food was good and plentiful. Lennie made me take cod liver oil because she said I was anemic, and this nasty stuff would increase my appetite, so I could gain some weight. The large serving spoon she used to serve the food for the restaurant was the same that she used to dose out the cod liver oil to me. She had it filled full of cod liver oil, and I had to drink a glass of orange juice with this stuff to get it down. Of course, you burped the oil all day.

One of Lennie's friends picked me up and took me to Sunday school. One of my teachers, Mrs. Rosa, read Bible stories to us and gave us coloring sheets to bring home, and she always gave us candy to eat. She was a wonderful, slim woman with a medium build, and she smiled all the time.

Ms. Rosa taught us Sunday school for years, always at the same church. Ms. Rosa never drove a car, and someone always picked her up and brought her to church. She also taught Bible Study during the week, and I understand she did this until she became ill and was placed in a nursing home not too far from Dillon; she remained there until her death.

Some of the members often mimicked Mrs. Rosa's way of worshipping in the church during service when they went home for their Sunday dinner. You see, Ms. Rosa praised God openly during the church service. When you do not know any better, you find humor in the way some people praise God. If we understood what she was doing, we would have been praising God with her. The Methodist Church worship service was always calm and serene.

Mr. Jude, another member, also gave praise to God by speaking loudly, and he ran around in the church and spun around like a whirlwind. He and Ms. Rosa had a good time praising God during Sunday service. Therefore, I guess Mr. Jude and Ms. Rosa were out of order.

The children in the church always had to sit in the front pew, in front of the adults. This was their way of making sure you behaved properly. We had to refrain from talking, chewing gum, eating, and giggling—and you had better not go to sleep. If you did, the adults sitting behind you thumped you on the back of your head or maybe pulled your ear or tapped you on your shoulder to let you know that you were in trouble.

Many professional people, such as teachers and even the black doctor and his family, were members of this church. I remember as a child, people often said rich blacks went to the Methodist Church.

Mother Emma's church, which was the Baptist Church across town, had a lively service, with a lot of hand-clapping, singing of praise songs, and shouting in the spirit. The style of worship was completely different. The members shouted and had a good time, and their service was longer.

Mother Emma's Pastor, Rev. Gusset, talked about the women wearing bright, red lipstick and pink blush on their cheeks. He spoke about the kind of clothes they weren't supposed to wear— tight, short dresses and skirts—clothes that were too revealing. He spoke of how wearing these types of clothes sent you to hell, and women who dressed like that, adorned with lots of jewelry, were called Jezebels. Rev. Gusset talked about the people drinking the night before and coming to church with hangovers and falling asleep.

When I first moved to Dillon, of course, I didn't know anyone. Lennie had a good friend who had a large family, like my mama. Mrs. Sara's eldest daughter, Stephanie, was the first person whom I met after moving there. Her mother and Lennie were very good friends, and Lennie often let me go to their house to play. In fact, Mrs. Sara was a hair dresser, which she did in her home.

After awhile, Lennie had Mrs. Sara to take care of my hair. She washed and straightened my hair with a hot comb and curled the ends and then put it in a ponytail.

I guess by now my mama and grandma decided it would be to my advantage to continue to live with Lennie and her family. It did not look like I was going back to live with them anymore. They wanted me to go to school and have a better life. Since my stepfather had already tried to molest me that one time, there was nothing to say that he would not have tried again.

Lennie and her family were good to me. I was meeting people, and doing things that I would not be doing if I were still living with my birth family. I guess with me being as young as I was, I did not understand why I was sent away to live with someone else. I never heard anyone refer to each other as black or white. I did not know that there were places that blacks could not go, and I did not know why. As a child, we learned by listening and doing what we were told to do and observing the behavior of others who were older and wiser; I call this learned behavior.

Lennie and Mother Emma were fair-skinned people, so I did not have a problem blending in as part of their family. I could have belonged to someone in her family, as far as the people from Dillon were concerned; however, they knew I was not her child.

I was talking with my sister recently, and, in our conversation, I learned that my grandma was the one who insisted that I live with Lennie and her family. My mama was not happy about me leaving to live somewhere else—what mother would be?

I missed my family, especially my brothers and my sister, but there was always something going on at the juke joint downstairs on the weekends to keep my mind occupied. There were no kids to play with at Lennie's house, and it was hard having kids over because there was no place to play. You see, we were right in front of the railroad track, so there was no front or backyard. She did not have a living room, so we could not sit and play there, either. There were no televisions back then, so we entertained ourselves by listening to the stories on the radio, such as *The Lone Ranger, Sky King, Amos and Andy, Dell Evans and Roy Rogers.* In addition, we read many comic books, and we had paper dolls to play with—some were bought, and some we cut out of the Sears and Roebuck catalog.

MY FIRST TIME GOING TO SCHOOL IN DILLON

It was a Monday morning, and I was excited because I was getting ready to start school. Lennie enrolled me in the elementary school, which was a black school that was across town. She bought me a new book bag, paper, and pencils, and she gave me a snack. I was dressed in one of the dresses that she had bought for me to wear to school, and, for the first time, at the age of eight years old, I was going to experience my first day going to school—except for the time I lived with the other family in North Carolina.

I probably walked with Stephanie to school. I was in the fourth grade, and my teacher was Ms. Watson, who was a pretty lady who wore glasses; she was nice.

The school day started at eight o'clock in the morning, and we were out at twelve o'clock noon. The reason we only went to school for half a day was because we were on split shifts. This was the only school for blacks, and, in order for everyone to go to school, we had to split the day in half. The high school students went in the afternoon.

I was happy to be in school; I would learn how to read, write, and do arithmetic. I had gotten books and a reader and had to practice my writing and learn how to add and subtract. This was exciting to me because I had almost missed out on an education because I didn't look white enough; I wasn't born black; and I lived during a time when things were separate, not equal.

As a young child in the early fifties, I was not aware of what was right and what was wrong as far as where blacks were allowed to go. I didn't know then that blacks and whites were separate in every since of the word. I was not exposed to some of the things the people did in Dillon. I was born in South Carolina, maybe sixty miles from Dillon. I guess because I was so young, I did not hear racial slurs. I was around white people all the time. They were my family, and if I did hear racial slurs, maybe I was not aware of what they meant.

In Dillon, as well as the other surrounding Southern areas, everything was segregated. When this is what you are exposed to, you learn to accept this way of life. Adults knew the difference because some of their parents or grandparents were born or grew up during slavery, which meant they were aware of the taboos of segregation. However, as a child growing up in the environment as it was, I didn't really see a difference between the races; it was not discussed around us until we were older.

The kids in Dillon didn't ask where I came from or who I was kin to. Some parents knew or thought they knew where I came from, because I learned later that many people, including teachers that came from Dillon, had visited my grandma on occasion.

Lennie often took me back to visit my family, and she saw my grandma while we were there—I guess to get her potions. This would give me time to spend with my brothers, my sister and my mama. I took them candy and cookies that Lennie had given me to take to them. We played and had fun; then, it was time to leave. I really missed them when I left.

As I got older, Lennie said to me, "Don't you tell people where you came from or who your family is, do you hear me? They can't come see you either, because the KKK will burn a cross in my yard if they find out that your family is white, and you are living with a black family."

I mention the movies a lot because that is all we had to do, except go to church, school, the joints, the fair or carnivals during the year, and each other's homes. I was talking with a friend of mine awhile ago, and she reminded me about this usual event that happened in Dillon when we were kids. The Goat Man came to town with all of his goats. There was a goat that pulled a wagon that the man had stuff on, and there were Billy goats and nanny goats. What's the difference? Who knows? We were excited to see him coming to town, and they smelled awful! The Goat Man traveled from the South on highway 301 going north somewhere we didn't know; we just knew he was passing through, and this was something to see.

Now, back to the movies. There was a movie theatre that we could go to as long as we sat upstairs. It only cost us twenty cents to get in. You had to go across the street to the train station if you needed to use the bathroom—if it was open. The kids would use the back of the balcony in the theatre sometimes as the bathroom.

Sometimes, school was fun. We had recess; we jumped rope, and I learned how to jump double dutch. We played hopscotch and softball, and we would shoot marbles; we had all kinds of pretty colorful marbles that we carried in a little sack. Sometimes, we had classroom jam sessions (played records and danced) and sold hot dogs.

Some afternoons, we had choir practice or Methodist youth fellowship meetings at the church or the church parsonage. The pastor's wife served us refreshments most of the time. I was in the children's choir. I met more kids who were nice, and I became friends with a lot of them.

On some Saturday nights, I went to the drive-in movie with the Rushmores, a family who were friends of Lennie's; they had a son named Chris. I had never been to a drive-in or movie theatre until I went to live with Lennie. Going to the drive-in meant you had to have a car to sit in and watch the movie on a large screen. This drive-in was for black and white people. The blacks had two rows in the front of the drive-in, which was very close to the screen. The section where the whites parked was bigger, and I am sure a lot easier for them to see the screen. There was a speaker that hung from a wooden pole that you placed in your car to hear the sound from the movie. Going to the drive-in movie was better than staying upstairs at the restaurant, sitting by the window and looking down at the people standing around outside the restaurant.

There was a place down the street from Lennie's called Bop City, where the teenagers gathered on Sunday afternoons. They danced and socialized with their friends. I was not allowed to go; I guess Lennie thought I was too young. Some of the kids I went to school with did go there. They danced and hung out with their friends and boyfriends. I was allowed to ride my bike there to buy an ice cream cone and back.

Lennie had a good friend who lived in another part of the town, and we visited often. Her friend, Ms. Simmons, sewed clothes for people and for me, as well. I was thin, and Lennie had problems buying clothes for me that would fit. I helped her lay patterns, pin and cut them out, and then I sat and watched her sew.

My mama sewed also. Remember I told you she made dresses for me and my sister out of flower sacks? The material was probably cotton and had lots of flowers, or there was some kind of print on it. I guess I learned that skill from her. I soon learned how to sew and could sew well. I learned how to make gathered skirts with a waistband—you sew a stitch and pull a thread to kind of bunch up the fabric, and then you attach a band around the skirt. In addition, I learned to make dresses. The gathers made me look thicker. These skirts are what I wore to school most of the time. We could not or did not wear pants to school. I do not know why—we just did not.

Mrs. Simmons was a tall, robust woman, maybe five foot nine. She was light skinned, and, really, she could have passed for white. She had straight hair that was salt-and-pepper colored. She wore glasses and lived in a very nice house with her sister. They were wonderful people and always welcomed me in their home.

I remember one time, Lennie, Mrs. Nora, and Ms. Elfie let Chris, Susan, and me ride a train called the Boll Weevil (Seaboard) to a small place called Little Rock to visit with friends of theirs. "You children sit in your seats and don't move until you get to Little Rock." They told us that someone would be there to pick us up from the train. Of course, we were a little scared traveling by ourselves, but we really had each other. When we arrived at our destination, one of Lennie's friends was there to get us.

Mrs. Farrell was waiting for us. "Hello children. Did you enjoy your ride on the train?"

Chris answered, "Yes ma'am, we did." She took us home with her, and we made sandwiches and she gave us each a glass of lemonade. We played in the yard on the swing that she had. Eventually, Mrs. Farrell's son told us it was time to take us home, which ended our day of adventure. What an experience!

PUBLIC AND PRIVATE
HIGH SCHOOL

When we were promoted to the eighth grade, we had to go to the new high school that was built for colored kids. We had to ride the bus because it was too far to walk. I walked to the Baptist Church, which was the bus stop for me; it was probably about three blocks from where I lived. Sometimes, if I was early and it was raining, I would go across the railroad track and catch the bus.

However, at the bus stop, there were many kids older than I was, and some were my classmates. Sometimes it would be very cold; they would build a fire in a big tin barrel, and we would stand around that barrel to keep warm. Sometimes, a teacher passed by in a car and gave some of us a ride.

I guess Lennie no longer needed my grandma, because we did not go back that much. Either that or she went when I was in school. I still missed my brothers. (My mama would write letters.) I had one brother who was born a few months after I left, in 1950. Therefore, I did not know him, and he did not know me. The times I went back to visit, my sister was not there; she had gotten married and lived in another town. However, I did see my brothers and enjoyed spending time with them.

Being in high school was different from being in the elementary school. We had homeroom classes, and we had to change classes when the bell rang. We had different teachers, depending on what classes we took. We stayed in school all day. In addition to that, we had a cafeteria, which allowed us to eat a hot lunch—that was great. We had a school band that I joined and played the drums. We had to wear blue pants and white shirts or blouses. Lennie could not find pants to fit me because I had long legs and I was thin. She went to a local department store and bought a pair of boy's pants that worked out just fine.

I also played basketball . . . well; let's say I was on the team. As I said, I was teased because we had to wear shorts, and I was thin. I was called bony maroni, Olive Oil (Popeye's girlfriend), string bean, as well as red bone, and high yellow. I did not care at that time, because I wanted to be on the team.

Even back then, people said things to hurt your feelings, and sometimes these things stayed with you as you got older. Teasing had a way of lowering one's self esteem. But we didn't know anything about that—at least I didn't. I wasn't aware of the effect it would have on me in later years. When teasing becomes a constant thing to some people, like me, I became shy and quiet. I didn't have the confidence that some of my friends had, that is, being out spoken. I was withdrawn and didn't feel good about myself.

In the new high school, we were given used textbooks from the white school. The whites received new textbooks. Because we were not given new textbooks, we were behind in the current information that we also needed to further our studies and be prepared for future endeavors.

In a building downtown on Main Street, we had a small public library. We had one in the new school, as well, which was great because we could check out books to read. In this building, there was a black beauty shop, and the black doctor had an office there, as well; I think he owned the building.

Dr. Brown was also a member of the Methodist Church. I remember him because I was anemic, and Lennie would take me to see him. I honestly believe he thought giving you a shot in your rear end with the biggest needle in the world was the cure for everything, because that is what you got when you went to see him.

Some Friday afternoons when I got home from school, my chore was to help Mother Emma scale and clean fish. Lennie bought fish by the crate, and our job was to see that they were cleaned and ready for her to cook for her customers on Friday nights and Saturdays. I probably smelled like fish when I went to the games on Friday nights. Since we did not have indoor plumbing, and there was no place to take a shower or a bath, we did the wash up thing.

There were times that Mother Emma visited with one of her friends who lived down the street from Lennie's on occasion. One night, it was getting dark, and I was in the place by myself. I was upstairs, and I remember Mother Emma calling me, and I answered, "Yes, Mother Emma, I'm coming." I ran down the stairs to let her in, but when I got there and opened the door, I looked out and she was not there. I was a little scared because I was sure she called me. Shortly after I had gone back upstairs, she called me again, and, this time, she was at the door.

I told her what happened, and she told me, "That was my spirit, letting you know that I was on my way."

Another time in this same building, Mother Emma had a friend who lived in the country that she would visit for a few days. I did not like it when she did this, because I had to sleep by myself and that was scary. One night I woke up, and saw a man with a black suit and hat on standing in the doorway. I started screaming and sat up in the bed. Lennie came in the room. "Girl what's wrong with you screaming like you crazy?" When I told her, she said, "You better go back to sleep and stop your foolishness."

Sometimes, I dreamed of a skeleton in the doorway hanging by its neck. Now, when Mother Emma was there, I never had these visions. I was told later that someone had been killed in the building before Lennie and her family moved in there.

Lennie had a partial bathroom built onto the back of the building that meant we did not have to use the outhouse during the day. However, at night we still used the slop jar.

There was this man, Mr. Brady, a black barber who drove a black Studebaker who came to the restaurant on Friday nights. He was a friend of Lennie's, and he would come upstairs as though he lived there, sat down in the big easy chair that was at the top of the stairs, and watched the fights. We could only get one channel, so it did not matter if we wanted to watch something. (Oh, I did not tell you, we finally got a television—black and white, since there were no color televisions, yet). If you wanted color, you could buy a sheet of blue plastic and cover the screen, and it appeared that you had color. Anyway, Lennie fixed him steaks and different kinds of food, and he sat there in that chair, eating and watching the fights.

Sometimes, he would come around twelve o'clock noon and sometimes in the evenings around five o'clock. He always ate in the dining room if he came during the day. I did not like him because he was fresh, and I did not like the way he smiled. He approached me one time and said, "Come here girl, and give me a kiss!" I always ran away from him. No, I did not tell Lennie; I did not think she would believe me, anyway. This is how kids are molested and do not tell, because they assume no one would believe them. He was always grinning, and he smoked and smelled like cigars.

I saw some pictures she had taken when the two of them had been to the beach; they had on bathing suits and were posing for the camera. I did not understand what was going on. Therefore, I decided to write her husband a letter telling him about the pictures and Mr. Brady. I slide the letter under their bedroom door, not realizing that Lennie would end up with the letter.

Of course, her husband never got it. When she found the letter, she said, "You have no idea what you have done!" I knew from the sound of her voice that she was upset with me. Yes, I was scared. I thought I was going to get a whipping, which I had not gotten before. Lennie lectured me by telling me that I could have caused a lot of trouble. What did I know, I was only a kid, and I thought her husband should know that this man was spending a lot of time with Lennie at the joint eating and watching television, as well as going to the beach. She didn't treat me as well after that; I guess I deserved to be treated that way because of what I did.

We eventually moved into the new restaurant that she and her husband built, which was down the street from the building we lived in before. One day, she said to me, "You will have to work to pay for your school clothes and supplies, because I am not going to anymore." When I asked her why, she told me, "Your mama didn't want you because she was with a colored man and had you; you're a half breed and you're ugly. I raised you, now you will have to take care of yourself, you understand me?"

"No, I don't understand what you are saying to me," I replied.

She said, "Whether you do or not, that's the way it is." I was in the eighth grade at the time. However, she got a job for me, working for a white family, cleaning house and ironing their clothes. The woman of the family had special dishes for me to use if I ate or drank water, and there was a separate bathroom for the help. I went to work in the morning and for the better part of the day, and then I had to work in the restaurant for the remainder of the day and evening. Whatever, Lennie wanted, that's what I had to do.

I think I made about $1.50 a day. I worked there for part of the summer, and then I started working in a diner downtown owned by relatives of the family whose house I cleaned. In this diner, I washed dishes and had to mix the table scraps in a big pot for the dogs. I don't know how much I made per hour, probably the same amount as the house I cleaned.

I worked there after school. They did not cook the kind of food I was used to eating. They were not Southerners. So, sometimes, they gave me a plate of some kind of beef stew cooked with tomatoes and rice; it was not bad.

I still had to work in the restaurant as well; sometimes late into the night or until Lennie was ready for me to go to bed. I had to get up at six in the morning to help clean the restaurant and sweep the front yard, wash the large picture windows, and help Lennie get ready for the next day. This was mostly during the summer, and during school vacations, and, especially, on the weekends.

I had to save my money to buy school clothes and anything else that I needed for school. I bought material, and Mrs. Simmons told me she would help me make skirts and dresses for school. She did not like the way that Lennie was treating me and the things she was making me do, but she never said anything to her about it. She was, however, very nice to me and treated me special.

The new building we were now living in—the one that I mentioned earlier—was a one-story building. The restaurant was in the front of the building, and the living quarters was in the middle; and there were also three bedrooms, and a half-bath that were in the very back of the building that she would rent out.

In the living quarters, we had a living room, a full bathroom, and three bedrooms. We still had to use the restaurant kitchen to eat our meals. The living quarters were very nice. Lennie had wall-to-wall carpeting installed throughout the house. The living room was furnished with a white leather sofa, a couple of armed chairs, end tables, and a cocktail table in front of the sofa. Lennie had a lady come in to make her draperies and to hang them. She knew how to get what she wanted, and everything looked really nice. We didn't have a living room before or a full bathroom. I had my own room, Mother Emma had hers, and, of course, Lennie and her husband had theirs.

I didn't have those visions of seeing things like I did in the other place we lived, but when I went to sleep, I could feel something come into the room and sit down across my legs. I couldn't move or say anything for a little while; then, I could feel it get up and leave. This happened often. I did tell Mother Emma, and she said it was spirits visiting me.

In September at the beginning of the school year, we had what they called the "Skillet Fair," which was organized by a group of men who lived in an area outside of Dillon, but still technically in Dillon County; the fair lasted for a week or so. This fair consisted of carnival rides, the Ferris wheel, merry-go-round, swings, and other kinds of rides. There was a place that we could go and play the juke box and dance and have fun with other kids with whom we went to school. There were special times set aside for the schools to bring the students in the afternoon; we were given admission tickets to get into the fair. This fair was for the black people in Dillon County, because we were living in segregated times. At night, during the week, families came and enjoyed the rides and good food. The best time was on the weekends, because just about everybody was there.

I had never been to a fair before, so I was overwhelmed. Some of the organizers were farmers, and they had homemade quilts, preserves, pies, cakes, ice cream, and even stands where they sold hot dogs, hamburgers, fresh barbecue, and other types of food. Of course, we could buy cotton candy and red candy apples, and there were booths where you could take a chance to win stuffed animals and other unique prizes.

There was the Minturn Picnic that was held on the opposite side of Dillon at a different time of the year, but I wasn't familiar with that. I think I went one time, but this wasn't as big as the "Skillet Fair." There were a lot of booths that sold all kinds of food, and the people gathered and had a good time. The Minturn Picnic lasted for a week.

During school, for trips, we often went to Atlantic Beach in South Carolina. This was the colored beach, and it was separated by a bridge between Myrtle and Atlantic Beaches. We were not allowed to go beyond the bridge, because that was the mark that divided the beaches. We often went to the beach on school, church, and other club groups for trips of enjoyment. We also went to Brook Green Garden, which was a garden that consisted of concrete statues of people and animals of different kinds, as well as flowers.

Atlantic Beach had hotels and stands where you could dance, buy food, and spend the night if you could afford it. Dillon was only about one hour and a half away. Most families who went to the beach took their own food, such as delicious potato salad, fried chicken, bologna, and peanut butter sandwiches and slices of pound cake and sodas to drink for the children and beer for the adults. We went in the water and had fun running from the waves. We either kept on the wet clothes or went in the cars and changed; there were no places to change unless your family rented a room to use. Once again, I was exposed to things that were new to me, and I loved it!

A good friend of mine had been attending a boarding school in South Carolina for at least a year. Her mother, Mrs. Morgan, must have given Lennie information about the school because one morning, Lennie came to me and said, "We need to pack your clothes because you are going to boarding school." I was in the eleventh grade at the time and had only been in school probably one or maybe two weeks. I had only been at the new high school three years.

Lennie woke me up and said, "Come on, it's time to go!" I was wondering, *where are you taking me?* She, along with a friend of hers, took me to the boarding school in South Carolina. When we got there, I was once again scared. I didn't know what was going on or what was going too happened. Lennie went inside a building, and, after awhile, she came out and said, "I'll have to bring you back because they have no available rooms, and you can't stay." Well, we went back to Dillon, and I was kind of glad because I had no idea what she was doing or why.

I returned to the school in Dillon and started the eleventh grade. I had my class schedule, and I thought everything was going well. Probably a week or so into the school year, early one Sunday morning, Lennie came into my room and woke me up to tell me that I needed to pack my clothes. I thought to myself, *here we go again*.

She told me, "Pack your clothes; I'm taking you to Laurinburg to boarding school!"

Okay! You have really given me plenty of time to get it together, I thought to myself.

After packing what clothes I had, she said, "I'll send what you can't pack; come on, let's go." After getting dressed and eating some breakfast, we left. I had never been to Laurinburg before and didn't know it was in North Carolina.

After what seemed to be a long ride down the rode, we finally reached this place that had several one-story brick buildings; they were actually quite nice. She didn't drive; she had someone to take us to the school. Apparently, she had taken care of my admission and everything ahead of time, because she helped put my clothes in the room and took the empty suitcases with her and left.

I didn't know anyone there, and, as I stood in front of the building that I would be living in, suddenly I felt so alone. She literally dumped me off and left. I was on my own. I met my roommate, who was from New York; this was her first time away from home, as well. It was time for dinner, so we went to the cafeteria where we were shown what to do, where to sit, and how to proceed with our dinner.

After eating, we went back to our rooms, and I began to meet some of the girls in the dorm. My roommate was nice and had only been there a few days before me. I was so alone, I cried most of the night. I don't know why I wasn't happy to be away from Lennie; after all, she wasn't nice to me anyway.

The next day, I started my classes and found that the guys in my class were a bunch of clowns; they thought everything about me was funny, from my name—because my last name was Stackhouse, I was called brick house or anything to get a laugh—to where I was from—because I was from Dillon, they called me Marshall Dillon (the western *Gunsmoke*). I was ridiculed for awhile in the classroom and dining room because these were the same guys I had to eat my meals with everyday. Actually, Josh, who was from New York and had been in the school for a few years, insisted on teasing me, but he was kind of cute and I had a crush on him. One day in the dining room, he gave me an envelope, and I thought it was a sweet note. I sat there and opened it to find out that he was playing a joke on me; the note said, "Wate on Tablets." He was making fun of me because I was so thin. Well, I was so embarrassed, I started to cry, and one of the guys said, "I told you not to do that!" I decided to ignore him after that and didn't say anything to him. Because I ignored him, he eventually stopped teasing me, and we became good friends.

Most of the students in the school were from New York, or New Jersey, and some were from Chicago, and North Carolina, I believe I was the only one from South Carolina.

I had gotten settled, and this was my new home for two years. A black couple who had an interest in educating young black children founded this private boarding school. They founded the school before integration (in 1904).

I did not like being there at first because once again I had to adjust to a new life, and this time I was pretty much on my own. I was in private school, hopefully, to get a better education, and this was to be my family for the next two years.

Being away in boarding school, your focus is on whether you can survive. Really, for me, it didn't matter and my thoughts were about getting along and adjusting. I had no thoughts of my biological family. There were no concerns about my racial background because it wasn't important anymore. It was the same situation as when I first went to Dillon to live; only I was older. I should have been happy to be in boarding school because I was finally away from Lennie.

We had a canteen where we could socialize after classes were over, and we could buy fried bologna sandwiches, which were very good, and we had chips and sodas.

We had to wear uniforms, which were gray skirts (pants, for boys) and blue blazers with the school emblem. A white shirt/blouse had to be worn with the uniform. We looked good in our uniforms, and we had to wear them on Sundays and anytime we were off campus. During the week, we wore regular clothes for classes. On campus, we had to wear the uniforms on Sundays for meals and our Christian Endeavor, which was a Christian service that was mandatory. This was our choir uniform also.

On Sundays at seven thirty in the morning, we were at breakfast; then, we had room inspection before leaving for Sunday school.

On Sunday mornings, the young men had to line up in front of the student center, and the dorm leaders had to do an inspection of their appearance before we were ready for Sunday school. After Sunday school, the girls got on the bus and went to a church in the community.

After church, we came back to the campus, and we had time to relax for awhile or visit with family, if they came. Then, at four o'clock, it was time for Christian Endeavor and then supper.

We didn't go home for the Thanksgiving holiday because the break was short and many of the students lived too far away; there was not a lot of time for traveling. Therefore, we had a great Thanksgiving dinner on campus. We went home for Christmas break, however, which was for three weeks.

It was almost time for Thanksgiving, and we had our Homecoming activities coming up. We had a parade, and we wore our band uniforms which were blue and gold. We didn't have much of a football team, but we had one. The homecoming queen had to be a senior, and I think we had a dance.

We had activities on campus: our Founders' Day, and roll call. We had a big dinner with turkey, dressing, vegetables, cranberry sauce, rolls, sweet potato pies, and other good stuff, and we did have plenty to eat.

The holiday was soon over, and it was time to begin another week. Some students were invited to the President's house to have dinner with him and his family; that was very special. After Thanksgiving, we started getting ready for the main event: our Christmas Cotillion. This was my first year, so I wasn't familiar with what they did. It was almost the same as getting ready for a prom, only bigger. We had to wear formal attire, and the recreation center had to be decorated, which the students did, and we had to learn how to ballroom dance. We actually ballroom danced as part of the cotillion; this was actually beautiful.

As time drew near, I told Lennie what I needed for the cotillion. A family friend of hers had a white, short, semiformal gown that she said, I could borrow. I think she brought it to me from Dillon or she mailed it; she probably mailed it. I don't think I went home for a weekend to get it. I bought some red chiffon material and made a skirt to wear over the bottom part of the dress. I did look nice in the red and white. Some of the girls' parents sent them beautiful, long gowns to wear with the matching shoes.

This was the biggest event on the campus. We had escorts, if you wanted one; however, we had to have one for the ballroom dance—after that, it didn't matter. I don't remember who escorted me during my junior year, but, we had a great time. After the cotillion, the students going to the Northern states were packed and ready to get on the buses that the school had chartered to take them home for the holidays. We were all sad because we didn't know who would be coming back.

Going home for three weeks was supposed to be a treat because we had not been home since before September. I think Lennie sent someone to get me because I don't remember her coming for me.

One of the first things I did after getting back to Dillon was to visit the school I once attended; of course, I wore my uniform and talked with all the teachers and some of the kids who were still there. Some had moved to the North with relatives. There were other kids' home from college and only two of us from a private boarding high school. We got together at each other's houses, played cards, and ate. I had to stay home and work in the restaurant, or sometimes, I was able to go to a friend's house and hang out with her and some other friends. If I did go anywhere, I had to be home by a certain time, and I wasn't allowed to go to the joints.

On Sunday at church, we had to participate in the student day program by telling who you were and where you went to school. Lennie seemed proud of the fact that I was standing there talking to the church people, telling them I went to boarding school.

She never came to the school to visit while I was there. It made her look good to the people in Dillon that I was in private school; although I did reap the benefits from being in a private school; I made some good friends, and I received an education.

The two years that I was there, I didn't keep in touch with my biological family, and Lennie never told me that she had heard from them. I guess, in a way, they were not on my mind at that time. Did I have thoughts of where I came from? Not really; I guess I didn't have time to think about it, and no one was concerned about me. With most of the kids from Northern states, they didn't have issues with segregation; the schools there were already mixed.

The holidays were over, and we knew it was time to go back to school and complete the year. It was good to be going back to see my roommate and my other friends. As I said before, we were still babes on campus and still learning. Graduation was in May, and we were sad to see some of the students that we had known for a long time leave the school. We would probably never see them again. This was the end of my junior year. In addition, I knew that I would be a senior the next year and would be getting ready to go away to college somewhere.

I don't know what I did that summer; I guess I stayed in Dillon and worked in the restaurant. When it was time to go back, though,

I was ready. My roommate came back, and we continued with our same activities: we were in the choir and still in the band, my roommate was a majorette and I continued with the clarinet.

This year, there were two of us from Dillon there. Remember Chris whose parents would pick me up on Saturday nights and take me to the drive-in-movie? They sent him to school there also. I tried to tell him how to get along with everyone, but he didn't want to hear what I had to say. I left him alone and saw him sometimes. I was a senior, and he was a junior.

He was in the band and played the trumpet—he did pretty well—and he was in the choir. Joining the choir was a special thing, not like the school glee clubs. The President of the school directed the choir, and his sister played the piano for us. Mr. Rosenthal taught us how to sing without music, and we learned how to harmonize. We had to learn discipline in order to follow his directions. We learned how long to hold a note, when to breath and how to do this together at his command. We were awesome. He was proud of us, and we represented the school very well. I was glad to be a part of the choir.

In the band, we had to practice a lot and learn our music. I had to play a clarinet because they would not let girls play the drums. When I was in Dillon, I played the snare drum. Our director graduated from A&T University in Greensboro, North Carolina, and not only was she our band director; she was our business teacher, and she was our dorm matron.

The band at the college she attended was fast, and they were high steppers, and that's what she taught us to do. I thought it was very neat. The best part was that we had to learn how to march.

I had a good class schedule; I was able to take typing and short-hand again, which I really liked. The typing was a challenge because we had blind keyboards (no letters on the keys). I often challenged Josh, because he took shorthand and typing, and he was really good.

We even had a junior sorority, which I joined and had a ball. The President of the school's daughter was away in college, and when she came back for holidays, she started this sorority for the girls. To be a part of the junior delta sorority, we had to apply by filling out an application and meeting certain criteria, and then we could meet with the leaders and get our instructions for the next step. We had to go through an initiation for a week before we were officially members of the junior sorority.

We had lady-like teas, where we had to learn the correct way to hold a cup and saucer with tea in the cup and a cookie on the saucer. We had to hold the napkin, cup, and saucer in our hands and not on a table or in our laps. These were things young ladies needed to know.

There were only two girls in the senior class, and one was to be queen for the Christmas Cotillion; I would be the homecoming queen. As homecoming queen, I wore a walking suit, which was blue tweed. I wore a hat and a fur stole around my shoulders, which belonged to the wife of the President of the school. I sat on the hood of a red car that was driven around the campus with a banner on it that read "Miss Homecoming" and "Miss Laurinburg Institute of 1961."

By the way, our choir was invited to Dillon to the Methodist Church that we grew up in to give a concert. I am sure Mrs. Rushmore, Chris's mother, and his sister had something to do with us coming.

We did good; as I said, we had an awesome choir. The church fed us as well, so you know the food was good and we enjoyed ourselves. I knew Lennie would be there; the performance was on a Sunday afternoon so it didn't interfere with her business.

Later in the year, our band was invited to participate in their (Dillon's) homecoming as well. We did well that year; we participated in many school homecomings, and we enjoyed being able to travel to other places.

In December, we had our Christmas Cotillion again and, of course, I had an escort this time—someone I could enjoy dancing with. His name was Jamal, he was from North Carolina, and he was somewhat of a clown. I don't know what I wore that year, probably the same gown. I know I had fun. We had a great time and, of course, we were ready to go home for the holiday. I think I went home with Chris and his family since they were going to Dillon. I knew Lennie was not picking me up.

What would make her be any different this time unless she was trying to impress someone? After getting home and settled in, I met up with my friend from the boarding school in South Carolina, and we hung out with other college friends whom we knew were home. We continued to visit each other's homes—except mine—ate good home-cooked food, played cards, and watched football games. Of course, the holidays always went by fast, and it was quickly time to return to school.

We continued with basketball season. There were a few new teachers—my shorthand and typing teacher for one. She was all right, but not as good as my first one. The guys did excellent, as always, in basketball. When it was time for graduation, I needed a white dress. I saved some money and bought some material and made my dress by hand. It turned out fine. No matter what was going on at school, Lennie just would not come through, and she did not come to my graduation—it was on the wrong day (Saturday), and her business came first.

Her husband came with a friend of theirs to pick me up the next day, and he brought my gift with him, which was a radio. I was grateful for the radio because I didn't have one.

MY FIRST SUMMER IN
NEW JERSEY

Lennie did not keep me around very long before she told me, "You are going to New Jersey on the train to stay with a friend of mine. Maybe you can get a job to help pay for clothes." This friend of hers had a niece who was a classmate of mine when I went to the public school in Dillon.

I was supposed to get a job and work for the summer, which I did not. This was my first time in the North, and I went to my friend's high school graduation. In the Northern states, things were integrated more than down South. My friend was graduating from an integrated school, which was new to me; I had not seen black and white students together.

Even though I was born into a white family, I didn't have any thoughts about race. I did not get a job and ended up going back to South Carolina. I was supposed to go to college in the fall. This was August, and the college I chose was the wrong one. I chose Florida A&M University, which is in Florida.

New Jersey was different from being down South because it was large, and there was public transportation like buses that took you to the places you needed to go. I remember, taking the bus to New York City, Manhattan, where the tall skyscrapers were, along with Macy's, Bloomingdale's, and the subways. I learned how to ride the subways and most importantly, I ate pizza. I had never had pizza before in my life. It was exciting and an experience for me being in New York and New Jersey even though I didn't get a job and had to return to Dillon.

MY YEAR AT DURHAM BUSINESS COLLEGE

I was told to choose a college somewhere else, probably because of the out-of-state fees. Well, all I had was an application to Durham Business College, and I thought that was a four-year college.

I didn't do my research, because if I had, I would have known that Durham Business College was a one-year school. I filled out the application, mailed it in, and was accepted in to the school.

I don't remember who took me to school; I probably rode the bus. We lived in boarding houses instead of dorms. In the house I was assigned to live in, I shared a room with three other girls, and they were all from Virginia. The twin beds were taken, so I had to share this big double bed with one of the other girls. We all became good friends and hung out from time to time.

They were smart and got very good grades. I did enough to get by, because I didn't want to be there. I made passing grades, but they were not as good as I could have done. We didn't have set rules, so we could leave whenever we wanted to as long as we were in at a reasonable hour. The women who owned the boarding house always cooked delicious meals for us.

Some of the guys who were students there had cars, and my roommates and I were friends with them so we were given rides to town on occasion. I realized I only had a year there, and I was looking forward to going to a four-year school, preferably North Carolina Central, which was in Durham, or A&T in Greensboro, North Carolina. I learned later that I wasn't going to continue my education; Lennie had falsely built up my hopes.

Anyway, I don't want to get ahead of myself. Thanksgiving came around, and I caught the bus to Dillon. This was my first Thanksgiving home because when I was in boarding school, we had to stay on campus.

When we returned to school, we shared family news about our holiday. Some of the girls brought plenty of food back, and some of them had new clothes. I rode the bus back to school; therefore, I definitely didn't bring food back or new clothes.

My roommates had sisters and brothers; I told them I was an only child, which I was in my adopted family. I never said anything about my family, and I didn't keep in touch with them anymore. I had adjusted to my new world quite well. After studying and taking tests, we went to basketball games, and downtown, and, sometimes, we went to the movies.

I joined the NAACP to be part of the demonstrations that were taking place in Durham; we were trying to eliminate segregation. The students started talking about picketing downtown at the theatres. I joined one of the picket lines and carried picket signs back and forth in front of the theatre. We were told to ignore all remarks that were made by anyone who was trying to break the picket lines.

We were called all kind of names, and sometimes they would push us off the street and throw things, like ice-cold sodas. We had to ignore them and continue walking. Sometimes, we were even spit on (these were white people who did these things). It never dawned on me that this was the race I was born into and that they were objecting to mixing with a minority group of people, which I was now part of. They would do anything to get us to break the line. We had to stand strong and keep picketing.

One of my roommates, Jackie, was sitting on the inside of the window ledge one weekend when these guys passed by in a car. One of them saw her, had the guys to stop the car, and asked for the girl who was sitting in the window upstairs. When she went downstairs to see what he wanted, he told her who he was, and that he was going to marry her. Not only did that blow her mind, but ours, too.

The young man came back, and they dated for awhile. We found out that he was stationed at Fort Bragg. He proposed to Jackie, and they eloped and were married before graduation. Her parents didn't know she was married until after graduation. Jackie was from Virginia, and she was very smart and an attractive girl. She was happy and we were happy for her. The only thing we were interested in was graduating and going home. I didn't think much about Jackie getting married; she found the love of her life and he was a nice guy.

It was time for graduation and, of course, the ceremony was on a Saturday. I received my diploma and shared those happy moments with my friends because Lennie wasn't there. She came up that Sunday, and you would never believe who drove her to Durham—Chris, the guy from Dillon and from boarding school. I was shocked to see her because I thought I would have to ride the bus home, even though I had a lot of stuff to transport.

MY FIRST JOB
AFTER COLLEGE

After leaving Durham and going back to Dillon, I stayed for a short while before accepting a secretarial job at my old high school alma mater. I was excited about returning. There were still a lot of people there whom I knew, and my job was rather easy.

I lived in the dorm for awhile, and I was told that they needed more rooms for the girls, so they added a mobile home to the campus. I had never stayed in a mobile home before, so I didn't know that they were not very secure; it rocked if it was very windy. I was asked to live there with some of the girls. I did not, however, like living there, because it wasn't secure, and there was too much movement. I didn't feel safe when we had bad weather. Eventually, they moved the girls back into the dorm, and I went with them.

I enjoyed working at the school and stayed there for a year. I worked for summer school and learned later that Chris was there in summer school, as well—not because he failed. In fact, he graduated from private school with honors and was valedictorian of his class.

Chris went to summer school to a black college, and he enrolled in classes with graduate students; the classes were a serious challenge for him. Therefore, he asked to come home, which he did, and his parents sent him to our alma mater for the summer school program, probably to get him out of Dillon.

Chris was dating Diane, a girl who lived in the city when he was in boarding school. Diane was a pretty girl, who had dated Norton, a student my first year at boarding school for two years. He told me that Diane graduated from high school and went to college in Durham, where she met and married a guy who was stationed at Fort Bragg. I think Chris found out after the fact.

During my stay at my alma mater, I decided to get my driver's license so that I would be able to drive the station wagon that belonged to the school. I went to the license bureau, I applied for my license, and I completed the road test and passed everything. Anyway, they wanted to see my birth certificate for verification of my age. In the meantime, I contacted Lennie and told her that I need my birth certificate. She mailed my original birth certificate to me, and I took it to the license bureau. The man looked at it and said, "We can't accept this document because it has been tampered with!"

"Sir, what's wrong with it?" I asked. He told me that someone had tried to remove the race and had written something different.

Lennie, apparently, used bleach to remove the word "white," which was my race on that birth certificate, and wrote "colored" in the space. I sent the paper back to her and told her what they said. Sometime later, I got mail from her; it was my new birth certificate. I paid no attention to the birth certificate after she sent it to me. When I went to the license bureau to give them my birth certificate so I could get my drivers license, there was no problem; they accepted the document and issued my license. What I didn't know was that this same birth certificate was going to create a problem for me later.

I continued to work at my alma mater for a year, when Lennie contacted me to let me know that my old roommate, Joyce's, mother, had contacted her to ask if she thought I would be willing to come to New York to stay with Joyce for awhile. I was ready for a change, so I told her that I would come. I needed to notify the school to let them know that I would be leaving.

MY SUMMER WITH JOYCE IN NEW YORK

I packed my clothes and took the train to Queens, New York. Joyce's mother, Mrs. Cora, met me at the station in Queens and we went to her house, where Joyce and her daughter, Gwen, lived with her mother and stepfather.

Joyce had the cutest little girl, who was not quiet a year old. Mrs. Cora told me that Joyce was planning to get an apartment in Brooklyn, and she didn't want her to live there with Gwen by herself. Joyce was raised in Queens and had friends who lived in Brooklyn. Joyce's mother took us to Brooklyn and helped us get settled.

This was a one-bedroom apartment on Fulton Street. I knew this was not what Joyce was accustomed to, and I was surprised she was settling for less. We were in a second- or third-floor apartment. The apartment had a kitchen with an eat-in dining room, living room, a bedroom, and a bathroom.

We had a crib for Gwen and a set of twin mattress in the bedroom. I slept on the box spring, and Joyce slept on the mattress, which was situated on the floor. The apartment was infested with roaches. At night, when we turned the lights off, the roaches came out in full force. We couldn't leave any kind of food out because the roaches would claim it. Joyce even had to cover Gwen's bottle to keep the roaches away from it. When we went to bed, I promise you that I could feel roaches being crushed under my body whenever I rolled over. I was used to roaches because Lennie had them in her place, but not to the point where they ruled the place. She did have an exterminator to come in on occasion.

I don't know why Joyce didn't go to college; she could have because she was very smart. She was, however, on assistance in New York with a small baby. While I was living with Joyce, some friends from Dillon were planning to come to Brooklyn, and they asked Lennie for my address. One day while we were sitting around, they came by. I was glad to see them, and after introducing them to Joyce, we talked about what they were doing in Brooklyn. Mrs. Elfie had family who lived in the same area as Joyce and me. Ms. Elfie was one of my teachers from Dillon when I was there in high school. She was with her cousin Susan, who also attended the same boarding school that Joyce and I did.

Susan told me she was working with another friend from Dillon, and they both had jobs in Long Island, New York, doing sleep-in work. She told me she could get a job for me if I were interested. I hated to leave Joyce, but I needed to make some money. Joyce didn't need to live like that anymore, especially with a small baby; it wasn't safe for her. We contacted Mrs. Cora, Joyce's mother, and I told her I was going with Ms. Elfie and Susan and that I was going to get a job in Long Island, doing sleep-in work.

I hated to leave my roommate, and I hoped she would be all right. I learned later that Joyce's mother came and took her and Gwen back to Queens. I kept in touch with Joyce—she was doing find; she had two little boys. The sad thing was that Gwen died when she was just a little girl, although I am not really sure what the cause of death was. I saw Joyce years later, and she told me that the boys were living with her dad in North Carolina and that she was dancing in the clubs in New York. That's the last time I heard from Joyce.

The sleep-in work was alright; I was doing general house cleaning for a family who lived in Hicksville, New York. It didn't work out, and so Sofia got me a job working with a different family, who was very nice. They knew I had a year of college and told me that I could do much better than housework. We stayed and worked for the remainder of the summer, and then we went back to Dillon.

MY RETURN TO DILLON

The summer was over, and we returned to Dillon. After being in Dillon for a short period of time, I was offered a job as secretary at the local black high school. Lennie seemed to be proud of me. She knew someone who had a car for sale, and she thought this would be a good car for me. She took me to the lady's house, and we bought the car. The arrangement was that the car would be in Lennie's name, and I was responsible for making the payments. However, I had to learn how to drive the car because it was a standard shift.

I was so excited that I had a car. Lennie showed me how to change the gears and told me, "You can practice driving the car on the street in front of the business." I finally learned how to drive it, and, I admit, I did really well. I visited with friends, and, most importantly, I drove to work.

I was involved with Sunday school at church and formed a dance group with some girls from the school. Everything was going so well. Lennie and I were getting along, and I still helped her with the restaurant and spent time with Mother Emma. I did not go out a lot because there was nowhere to go.

There was nothing else to do except work in the restaurant, and, of course, I had my job with the school. The theatre was up the street about a block or two, and, if I decided to go, Lennie told me, "You better be back by the time I turn my lights off." As soon as I would get up the street, I would look back, and she would have the light turned off.

After the movie, I had to knock on the door, because she locked it. I had to wait outside on the porch until she felt like letting me in. I did not have a key. She was just mean like that.

Sometimes, when I got home from work or anywhere else, if I wanted something to eat she would say "if you didn't buy any of that food, you don't eat." I would go to the grocery store next door and get sandwich meat and a loaf of bread to eat. Now mind you I weighed maybe ninety pounds so I did not need to miss any meals. But she let me know she didn't care, just depended on how she felt at the time. However, I continued to stay with her and of course, I had Mother Emma to talk to and laugh with.

Each payday, I gave Lennie money for the car. One day, she said, "Give me the keys to the car!" When I asked why, she replied," Don't question me; just give me the keys!" Well, I gave her the keys to the car.

I asked, "How am I supposed to get to work?"

"The best way you can," she replied. I didn't understand what she meant by what she said or what she was doing. I really didn't have a choice in the matter. The car was in her name, and there was nothing I could do. I rode to work with another teacher or whoever was willing to give me a ride there and back. There were times Lennie drove me to school, and I had to get back the best way I could. After I got paid, I made up my mind that I wasn't going to give her my money, since I couldn't drive the car, and I didn't even have a key.

She knew I had gotten paid and came to me. "Give me the money for the car!"

"No!" I told her.

"What did you say?"

"I can't drive the car," I responded, "so why should I give you my money?" She was furious.

"Girl, you don't know what you are doing!" Well, later that day, she and her husband came into my room. She told him that I wouldn't give her the money for the car and that he needed to beat me.

I was twenty-one years old when this took place. I was sitting on the bed in the room and didn't realize that he would really do what she told him to do. He went into the bathroom and came back with his razor strap that he used to sharpen the razor that he shaved with. He said, "You don't want to give Lennie her money for the car, huh? What's wrong with you?" He began to shorten the strap by winding it around his hand, and I thought to myself, *he really isn't going to hit me with that thing*. By that time, I saw him raise his hand over his head and that strap came down on my body. I knew, then, that this man was serious; he was actually going to beat me because she told him to. I tried to get off of the bed, but I couldn't. He raised his hand again and hit me continuously with that strap. Then, he decided to drop the strap and started hitting me with his fist and then with his open hand. I was finally able to get away from him and started running toward the door and out of the house into the street. I finally ran to a friend's house; it was a short distance away, but I made it. When I got there, I knocked on the door and explained to them what had happened. My friend, Morgan's, mother, Mrs. Houston, told me to stay there for the night and that she would help me the next day. With the help of a lawyer, I was able to get my clothes—Lennie would not give them to me otherwise. I stayed in Dillon for a short while, and my friend and I caught the train to New Jersey. I had friends there with whom I could stay for awhile.

I just left the job that I had with the school, and I heard all kind of stories about why I left in such a hurry. But I was embarrassed, and I knew I needed to get out of there and away from Lennie and her husband.

After living in New Jersey with Rochelle and Mason, friends of mine, I returned yet again to Dillon. There was a secretarial job in South Carolina, in another town not far from Dillon. I applied for it and was hired. I stayed on this job for almost a year.

I guess someone told Lennie where I was because she came to the town to see me, and I let her talk me into moving back to Dillon with her. She wanted me to help her take care of Mother Emma because of the stroke she had. She promised me that she would help me return to a four-year college if I still wanted to get my degree.

You learn from your mistakes, and this was a big one, because I believed her. She could be so convincing and sincere that I let her sucker me in hook, line, and sinker.

I went with Lennie back to Dillon and helped her take care of Mother Emma, who was paralyzed on her left side because of the stroke. I learned how to bathe and put her in her wheelchair, and sometimes, I pushed her outside for fresh air and sunshine.

Why did I go back to live with Lennie? I believed what she said, which didn't happen. I cared for Mother Emma, and I knew she needed someone to be there for her.

After Lennie rejected and abused me so many times, I should have kept going and never looked back. Whatever the drawing card was, I continued to hang around. I could have gone back to Society Hill, which I did not. I was a different person now. I was part of a different culture. So how would I fit in if I returned to my biological family?

I got a job as a secretary at an elementary school not too far from Dillon. Lennie made all the arrangements for me, as usual, including where I would stay and how I would get to work. Lennie took me to talk with Mrs. Livingston about rooming with her. She was a very nice lady; she was short, wore glasses, and had a very nice, neat house. Mrs. Livingston told me that I could room with her for fifty dollars a month. I would have to provide my own food, and I would have my own room. Since we worked at the same school, I could ride with her to work and back to the house. This was a good arrangement, and I was grateful. Then, I spent my weekends working in the restaurant in Dillon with Lennie.

I did this for awhile, and then I made my own arrangements. Mr. Jessie, a friend of the family, told me he would give me a ride to Mrs. Livingston's house, and he would pick me up at six in the morning, because this is when he was off work. This arrangement worked out just fine. I hated getting up so early in the morning, but I did what I felt I had to do. I had a good job, and I liked the people

I worked with. Lennie still had the Falcon, which she drove all of the time.

There was a family in Dillon, the Bakers, with whom I spent a lot of time. We were members of the same church and taught school together. They had a little girl named Frances whom I brought home sometimes for Sunday dinner. Lennie did not seem to have a problem with my bringing her home.

The Bakers had other children whom I took to the drive-in movies on Friday nights in their car. Sometimes, Mr. Baker took me home after bringing the children back from the movie. One night, he told me to take the car home and bring it back the next morning. When Lennie found that out, she told me to take it back to him and not to drive the car home again. She followed me to Mr. Baker's house to return their car.

Every now and then Lennie would let me drive the Falcon to run errands and to see Mrs. Simmons, the friend who sewed for everyone.

I did not hear from my family in Society Hill; I had not seen them for a long time, and I had not written to them. I do not know if Lennie was still going to my grandma's or not.

By now, I was still trying to figure out where I was going and what I was going to do. I really did not feel like I belonged anywhere, and I thought that I would be leaving Dillon soon; I would probably go back to New Jersey.

One day, I was on the other side of town, and I saw Chris, a guy with whom I went to boarding school. He had gotten taller, and he did not look like a nerd anymore, even though he still wore glasses.

Anyway, I was talking with my friend Alicia, and I asked her "Does Chris have a girlfriend?"

She said, "I don't know." Of course, when she saw him later, she told him I wanted to talk to him and that I wanted to know if he had a girlfriend.

Later that evening, Chris showed up at my house. I wasn't use to guys coming to visit me. Lennie never said it was okay for guys to come see me, and I never asked her. She knew Chris and his family, and I guess that's why she didn't say anything about him being there.

Chris was the type of person who didn't need to be invited; he assumed it was all right to show up. I was in the living quarters watching television with Mother Emma when he came by.

We sat and talked, and I asked him if he had a girlfriend. When he told me who she was, I was shocked to learn it was a mutual friend of ours from boarding school. I did not think she would date him, because he was not a sociable person and he was nerdy. Chris asked for a beer, and he wanted some chips and pork rinds with hot sauce, Lennie said it was okay to give it to him, so I did. He stayed for awhile and then left.

On occasion, we went to the movies and rode around town together. We talked about him being in school, and he wanted to know where I worked and what I did. I didn't see Chris too often; he only came by occasionally.

One day, Gloria, the girl whom Chris was dating, came to my house; she came from North Carolina. We were friends at boarding school, and Chris's sister, Angela, told her where I lived. I hadn't seen Gloria in years. She was with Faith, another friend of ours, and she was looking for Chris. When Gloria was talking about Chris, she said, "I just love him and want to know what happened; I haven't seen him." Unfortunately, I couldn't help her because I hadn't seen him, either. I wasn't in love with him; we just spent time together as friends.

Before she left, Gloria asked, "If you see Chris, will you tell him that I was here looking for him?"

"Of course, I'll tell him for you, if I see him," I replied.

A few days later, Chris came by my house and I told him that Gloria had been by looking for him. He didn't seem to be too excited about her visit; he just told me that he had gone to another town to visit with some of his cousins who attended the same college. I really didn't care where he had been.

Mother Emma's condition remained the same. She was not able to walk, but she could feed herself, and she loved to watch television. We sat and watched *I Love Lucy*; this was one of her favorite shows, not to mention *The Carol Burnett Show* and *Red Skeleton*. We laughed until we cried. These were precious moments; I will always cherish those times that I had with her.

As time went on, Lennie's moods constantly changed; one moment, she could be the nicest person and then sometimes, the least little thing triggered her off. One time, she was upset with her husband; he was sitting in a chair in the kitchen, and she took the dishcloth that she had, walked over to him, and slapped him on the side of his head with it. He jumped and asked her, "What did you do that for?"

She looked at him and replied, "You don't need to be sleeping in here; this is a place of business!" He was such a meek little man; he looked at her and walked out of the kitchen. I don't know where he went. She constantly fussed at him. He didn't have to do anything, and most of the time, he walked away. Yes, this is the same man who beat me before. He did what Lennie told him to do. I only saw him on the weekends and he never touched me again. I guess I forgave him for what he did to me and he seemed to be remorseful for what he did. I liked him, he was always nice to me, but I heard people say, he was hen-pecked, and I knew that wasn't the kind of husband that I wanted to have—if I ever had one. Strangely enough, I didn't know I was going to get one that tried to wring the hen's neck.

Chris and I did spend a lot of time together that summer, along with some other friends of ours. I have to admit we did have a lot of fun. He was in college, and he would be graduating the next summer. Because he was in ROTC, Chris had to attend summer camp at a nearby Air Force Base in South Carolina for a few weeks. I kind of missed him when he left, and he did write sometimes.

During the sixties, there was a draft, which meant the young men, upon graduating from high school, had to enroll in the selective service unless they went to college. Young men who went to college had to enroll in the ROTC program. The Vietnam War was going on then, and there were several guys from Dillon who were in that war. Some lost their lives over there. I didn't think about my brothers having to fight in the war.

I remember when Chris came to my house once; he asked me, "Where did you come from?" I told him that I was from Society Hill and that my family was white. He was surprised and asked, "Are you joking?"

"No, I'm not joking, and since you asked, I have five brothers and a sister that still live in Society Hill." I shocked myself, because I had never told anyone about my family. Lennie had told me not to, and I didn't until now. Chris never asked me anything else about my family, and I didn't tell Lennie that I had told him.

People in this small town knew I was not Lennie's daughter, and they knew she didn't have any children. You see, Lennie and her husband were successful business owners and respected citizens in Dillon, so was Chris's family.

After Chris went back to school in September for the fall semester, we decided to keep in touch, so we wrote to each other. During those days, there was more letter-writing than phone calls; everyone didn't have a phone, anyway. We had a pay phone in the restaurant.

After I returned to Lennie's, I suggested that we have a phone installed in the living quarters; she was alright with that as long as the phone was in her bedroom.

I still spent time with Mrs. Simmons the seamstress and tailor; she continued to help me with my sewing. When I visited with her, she talked a lot about Lennie and said she did not understand why she was so mean to me. She said Lennie was moody, and half the time we didn't know what to expect from her. Mrs. Simmons mentioned that Lennie often had gentlemen friends and asked me if I knew about them. I could tell she spent a lot of time with different men who came to the restaurant, but I didn't understand what that was about. Lennie was an attractive woman, and she was also quite flirtatious. Living with Lennie, I really saw more than I should have, and I think that was because of the type of business that she had. That could be why she was always sending me away, but she should have thought about that before she brought me to Dillon.

Time began to slip away from me, and I was still in Dillon, still dealing with Lennie, still doing the same things: going to work, going to church, and visiting with friends, and, of course, going to the movies and working in the restaurant until all hours of the morning.

But little did I know this would be my last year living in Dillon. I had already made up my mind that I was leaving, and I was going back to New Jersey where my closest friends lived.

Chris was in school, and his parents went to Washington every Thanksgiving. His father used to tease me all the time about his son and say that I was going to be his daughter-in-law; I don't know what made him think I would be interested in his son. But he would often tell me, when he came to Lennie's, that Chris was home. I didn't like his son. However, times had changed and I actually began to see Chris differently; he didn't look like a nerd anymore and I kinda liked him. We went to the movies and the recreation center with friends of ours to play cards and listen to music.

Anyway, I think it was October 13, in the early 1960s, when this gorgeous man died as a result of a truck accident on Highway 301 North, near Wilson, North Carolina. He was a truck driver, and, on his way home, his truck flipped; he did not survive. This was a sad time in Dillon. Many people liked Mr. Rushmore because he was a very kind man, and he could make you laugh. He and Lennie were very close; they were like brother and sister. I wasn't in Dillon when they had Mr. Rushmore's funeral. I know that Chris was heartbroken, and I was told that he wanted to leave school so he could take care of his mother; but she told him he needed to finish school because that is what his father would have wanted.

Anyway, back to that Thanksgiving in 1965. I rode with Chris's sister, Angela, and their family to Washington. I met Chris's Aunt Rosa, who was a robust woman and a good cook; she was a very lively person. I was not at Chris's Aunt Rosa's house that long. I was going to New Jersey from there to visit with my friends, Rochelle and Mason, who were also friends with Chris. They, too, were from Dillon. I always enjoyed spending time with them. Chris took me to the bus station, and I left for New Jersey.

It would soon be Christmas, and a lot of people would be coming to Dillon. Every year, from the time that I was a little girl, a group of black women in Dillon organized a dance every Christmas Eve (at midnight). This was a big event for the black people in Dillon. This was a formal affair with live music, and everyone looked forward to going. Not everyone could go; you had to be at least eighteen or out of high school in order to attend the dance. There were a lot of teachers and other professional people there, and they did not want the young people to see how they partied.

Some of us were old enough to go to the dance but decided to do something else. A group of us went to South of The Border, which is situated between the North Carolina and South Carolina line. South of the Border was owned by a man who was not from the South. He was one of the first to hire blacks as cashiers and waitress. Blacks could sit down and order their food and eat inside the establishment. This was the early sixties, during the segregation era.

During the holidays, Chris did come by the house, and he brought his books because he said he had some studying to do. He was studious and determined to get his studying done. He did not hang out like the rest of the college students. We sat in the living room while he did his homework. He did bring me Christmas gifts: a beautiful bracelet and some other things pertaining to the Air Force and his fraternity.

MY ENGAGEMENT AND WEDDING

Chris was graduating from college, and he asked me to come to his graduation with his family. I told Lennie I was going to Chris's graduation with his mother and sister, and she was fine with my going.

I told Mrs. Simmons that I was going to Chris's graduation and asked her to help me make two dresses. I had already made one dress; I bought the material, and she helped me make the other dress. I had two dresses to take with me: a light pink one and a yellow one. I had yellow dress shoes to match the dress.

I packed my clothes, and Lennie gave me a ham lettuce and tomato sandwich to eat on the trip. We had to stop at a rest area or gas station in order to eat because we could not eat in the restaurants. This was one of my favorite sandwiches. I carried that sandwich until we stopped, and the juice from the tomato and the grease from the ham had leaked, and the bag was greasy and wet. When we stopped, I foolishly dropped the bag in the trash because I was embarrassed. I still had chips and candy left to eat. But being embarrassed doesn't put food in the stomach; I wish I had kept my sandwich and eaten it.

We finally made it to Washington, D.C., and checked into a hotel called the Continental Inn. It was very nice, and there was enough room for all of us.

We had a quiet night after everyone was settled in, and we were up early the next morning when Chris came over to pick us up; he took us to their Aunt Rosa's house for breakfast.

After breakfast, we went to Chris's graduation ceremony, which was held outside on the campus. The weather was nice and not too hot. After the graduation ceremony, we went back to his Aunt Rosa's house and visited with her for awhile. Then we went back to the hotel and rested. We had to attend Chris's pinning ceremony, which was later that evening.

Chris presented me with a little box that had rings in it; his family did not know what he was doing, and I didn't either. I opened the box and there were two rings in it, an engagement ring and a wedding band. Chris put the engagement ring on my finger. I had no idea he was going to propose to me. Mrs. Nora, her cousin, Elfie, and Angela's husband were all surprised. They did not know that Chris and I had been dating—only Angela knew. She was the only one who knew that Chris was going to propose to me; she went with him to pick out the rings. I was happy and walking on a cloud.

We had to get ready to go to Chris's pinning ceremony. Students who were in ROTC were pinned with Second Lieutenant Bars, which meant they were now commissioned officers in the military—for Chris, it was the Air Force. I had the honor, along with his mother, Mrs. Nora, of pinning the bars on a tab on the shoulder of his uniform.

We then visited other family members in Washington. Chris introduced me to all of them, as well as some of their family in Maryland.

We returned to Dillon that Saturday evening. Chris took me home, and I shared my good news with Lennie, who was not excited at all that I was engaged to Chris. She told me that it did not mean anything, that I wasn't married to him yet, and engagements can be broken. I really loved her enthusiasm and happiness for me.

That Sunday morning, Chris picked me up, and we went to church together. The church had a small membership; in fact, this was the same church we both grew up in and where we would eventually have our wedding. Everyone knew each other, and, of course, most of them had known us since we were small kids. They were excited for us and wanted to know when the wedding was.

Chris took me to work that Monday morning, and my co-workers were excited and happy for Chris and me. We had to let everyone know that we were waiting to find out where Chris was going to be stationed before we made plans for a wedding.

Lennie's husband was happy that I was getting married, and he liked Chris, but he couldn't let Lennie know how he felt. He had to keep those feelings to himself in order to maintain peace with her.

Chris and I spent a lot of time together hanging out with his sister, Angela, and Alicia, a friend of ours, and her boyfriend, Arthur. We played cards, listened to music, and talked. We went to see the Bakers and Mrs. Simmons to share the news about our engagement.

I continued to visit with the Bakers and got a chance to spend time with Chris. After returning to Lennie's from the Bakers' one evening, Chris told me to drop him of at his mother's house and take the car home so I could drive myself to work the next day. He didn't need the car and at least he could sleep in if he wanted to. That was fine with me, but not with Lennie. When she saw his car in the driveway, she said, "You need to park that car on the street in front of the business!" The car was not blocking her car or anyone else's car, but because it was there for my use, she wanted it gone.

Mrs. Nora was passing by on her way home and saw Chris's car parked on the street. When she got home, she brought him back to pick up his car because she did not want it parked on the street. He picked me up the next morning and took me to work. Chris asked me why Lennie made me move the car. He had never seen that side of her. However, his family knew how Lennie could be. I told him I did not know that, she just did things like that; she didn't have to explain herself. Little did I know that he would end up being the same.

Anyway, Chris and I talked about having a small, family church wedding. The two families wanted to have a church wedding and that was that.

They started making plans—Angela, Elfie, Mrs. Nora, and Lennie. The first thing they did was make the guest list; I think they invited everyone in Dillon and Dillon County and other states and counties.

Lennie had her own ideas about what I was going to wear because she bought white satin material and had Mrs. Simmons to make a dress for me to wear for the wedding. It was short, and a line that was really pretty with a band of lace around the waist (an empire waistline). She bought a pair of white satin shoes to match.

Friends of Lennie's and Mrs. Nora's decided to give me a bridal shower at Lennie's. They decorated the room with colorful streamers that hung from a large umbrella that was covered with flowers made from colorful tissue paper. There were balloons of different colors everywhere. They had a table covered with a beautiful white linen tablecloth, and a table with a cake decorated with the words "Bridal Shower" in the center of the table. There were also refreshments, punch, various kinds of cookies and candies, and peanuts and mints that were arranged in beautiful crystal dishes. They had different colored paper plates, napkins, and cups that had silver wedding bells on them. The gifts were arranged on a different table with a white linen table cloth and flowers of different colors layered around the table. Several of our friends were there to help celebrate the bridal shower with me. We had a lot of laughs, and everyone had fun telling jokes of all kinds.

After the bridal shower was over, Lennie was her usual self. The ladies helped us clean, and everyone began to leave. Lennie started fussing about the gifts. "Why were the gifts taken to Nora's house instead of leaving them here?"

I told her, "We were trying to keep the gifts together and in one place." She didn't like the idea and became angry, which is when she grabbed me by the front of my blouse so hard the buttons popped off. Then she started hitting me and calling me a half-breed; she told me that I was no good and would never amount to anything. The only way I could get away from her was to crawl under the table in one of her dining rooms. I stayed under the table until she started to walk away and went into the kitchen.

She finally stopped fussing and sat down in the kitchen. This is when I quickly reached for the key on the wall that was inside of the kitchen door and went into the living quarters, hoping that she wasn't going to bother me anymore. I did go to bed praying that she would leave me alone.

Chris's sister Angela and their cousin Elfie continued making out the guest list, using the Dillon phone book. They invited several white people who were known on both sides of the family.

I guess this was a turning point in my life because I was getting married, and I was marrying someone whom I thought cared about and loved me. Chris's family had us pick out the invitations, which we did. Lennie was busy helping Mrs. Nora plan the wedding, deciding what color dresses the two of them would wear and the decorations for the church and reception.

A white friend of Lennie's owned a florist's shop and helped her with the flower arrangements for the church and for the bridal party. There was a wedding cake that Lennie had arranged to have done. I don't know who prepared the cake, but it was good and decorated beautifully with the bride and groom on the top.

The night before the wedding, Lennie prepared dinner for the bridal party at the restaurant on a Friday night. She was a good cook and really had a spread for everyone. She had smothered steak with gravy and onions, steamed rice, greens, peas, butter beans, home-made biscuits, fried chicken, and potato salad. She made sweet iced tea. There was a homemade peach cobbler and ice cream.

The ring bearer was the son of good friends of Lennie's and Mrs. Nora's; he was probably four or five years old. The flower girl was the daughter of friends of the family as well, and she was about three or four years old. We had two junior bride's maids, Fran, my little friend, and the little girl who lived across the street from Chris's mother. There were about seven ushers who were friends of mine and Chris's. My maid of honor was my friend Kathy from South Carolina.

Just before the wedding, Chris's mother, Mrs. Nora agreed to let us stay in one of the apartments she had across the street from her house; it was already furnished. I packed up what I had, which was clothes, a television, and a record player. We moved my belongings to the apartment on a Thursday. The apartment was very nice—there was one bedroom, a living room, an eat-in kitchen, and a full bathroom. Angela gave us some dishes and a few other things we were going to need for awhile. This is where I stayed with little Fran, my friend Katy, her brother, and his girlfriend until the wedding.

The week before the wedding, Angela took me to a dress shop in Dillon, on Main Street. The dress shop had the prettiest wedding gowns. Angela had a talk with me and told me that the dress Lennie had made for me was alright, but I should be getting married in a beautiful wedding dress with the veil and all the accessories.

I bought the prettiest wedding gown, with the veil, a long slip, and long, white gloves. I was so excited, I cried. I actually looked like a bride. Lennie did not know anything about the gown, and I was not going to tell her. I knew she would not want me to have the gown because she had given me the short one already and that was supposed to be good enough.

That Friday night, we had the wedding rehearsal at the church, and it turned out great. The wedding was on a Saturday evening. For the first time, Lennie was going to attend something that had to do with me. She didn't close the restaurant; there was some-one there who could run things until the wedding was over. There was nothing so important that she would close the doors for a day except on Sunday morning, when we went to church.

We had breakfast on Saturday morning; Lennie prepared it at the restaurant for everyone. We began to prepare for the wedding that afternoon, and Fran, the little girl who was with me, had gone home with her family because she had to get ready for the wedding. We received a lot of gifts from people around Dillon County and from other states as well; they had been taken to the church to be displayed where the reception was held.

That evening, my friend Kathy, my maid of honor, helped me get dressed. It was time to go to the church. It was a hot afternoon in the month of July, and after getting dressed, Kathy drove me to the church. After arriving at the church, there were cars everywhere and the church was full. Lennie's husband was standing in front of the church waiting for me and Kathy. When it was time, he took my arm and began walking down the aisle. This was a big, joyous day for us all.

The minister, Rev. Rogers, had not been at the church very long, and we were the first couple he married since he was ordained. He did a great job with the ceremony. Chris and I exchanged our vows before God. Rev. Rogers, who was as nervous as we were, pronounced us husband and wife; this was probably the happiest day of my life. Chris and I walked down the aisle and out of the front door to the reception, which was on the side of the church.

Lennie was surprised to see me walk down the aisle in that gown. When she had the chance, she said, "Where did you get that gown from?" I told her I bought it. She didn't say that I was a beautiful bride or that she was happy for me; she only asked where the dress came from.

After the ceremony, we took a lot of pictures in the church with family and the bridal party. Some of the church members and friends of both families displayed our gifts in the activity hall in the church, which had been beautifully decorated.

They had a table that was decorated with silver paper wedding bells, candles, and a large crystal punch bowl with some kind of punch made with ice cream, lots of cookies, nuts and mints. The center of the table was beautiful, with a three-tier wedding cake that had the bride and groom sitting on the very top. They took pictures of us cutting the cake and of course feeding each other the cake.

After greeting everyone, it was time to give our thanks and say our goodbye. Then we left the church. We went to Chris's mother's house and changed into casual clothes.

We did not go anywhere for the honeymoon because we were waiting for Chris to get his orders. That Sunday, we went to church and then we spent time with Chris's family. We were invited to eat dinner at this restaurant nearby; the owner was a good friend of both families.

During the coming week, I was still working. One evening after I had gotten home from work, Lennie came by the apartment yelling, "I want the money I spent on the wedding—my money for the flowers and cake!" She went on to say, "As far as I am concerned you're not married; I haven't seen any marriage license. I give you six months, and the marriage will be over!" That was the last time I saw Lennie, except when we got ready to leave for Colorado, which was a few weeks away. I really didn't have to listen to her anymore, and I certainly didn't need her permission to do anything.

SIX-MONTH TOUR IN COLORADO 1966 TO 1967

A few weeks later, Chris's orders came, and we started getting ready to leave for Colorado to go to the Air Force Base where Chris would be in school for six months.

We packed the car and rented a U-Haul to carry our clothes and some of our wedding gifts. Little did we know that Uncle Sam would have packed our things and shipped them for us. We said our goodbyes and began that long drive to Colorado.

It took us two days to drive through the country to Colorado. We stopped in Kentucky or Missouri, and spent the night in the Travel Lodge; I remember because of the little bears or koalas that were advertisements for those hotels. We ate dinner and breakfast at a restaurant that was across the street from the hotel.

We were not used to eating in diners or restaurants that were not black. We did not encounter any problems, however, and that was great, because we were hungry and wanted some good food.

We arrived in Denver, Colorado, the next day. Traveling through the country like we did was beautiful. Driving through the North Carolina mountains was awesome and yet scary. We were pulling a U-Haul behind the car, and the roads were winding and sometimes steep. But we had a great trip and had no problems with the weather or the car, at first. As we got closer to Colorado, however, we did begin having problems with the car; Chris started talking to the car, "come on, Blue Streak," which is what he called his car (because it was blue). What happened was that we had pulled too much on the transmission coming through the mountains and pulling that U-Haul trailer. But, we made it, and it didn't cost too much to get the car repaired.

Chris had a certain date to report to the base, and, actually, we were early. We checked into a motel, and Chris processed in and received all the papers we needed with travel pay. We were excited because we had some money.

We looked for an apartment and found one that was not far from the base. We had a furnished basement apartment with one-bedroom, a kitchen, and a living room with a small dining room. All we needed were dishes and personal items. We went on the base, and I got my military identification card, which made me a military dependent and allowed me to use the facilities on the base. We picked up other things that we were going to need from a place on the base that provided household items for families, or "military dependents."

We drove around and looked at the city of Denver, which was large and beautiful. The apartment we had was actually in a town called Aurora, which was near the base. Chris started school, and I began to look for a job. I joined a temporary agency, Kelly Girl, and they sent me to work with IBM as a temporary worker for six weeks. I really liked the job and met some wonderful people.

Some of the people I met were military dependents and some civilians. I made friends with some of them, and we went bowling and horseback riding. It was my first time horseback riding, and it was an interesting experience, especially if you have never been on a horse before; when you get off the horse, you have a hard time walking.

We decided to visit Pike's Peak, which I think is 14,000 feet above sea level, and Seven Falls' that had about 350 steps that you had to climb to get to the top of the fall, which had the most breathtaking view of the seven falls.

We were invited to dinner with some of Chris's classmates and their wives. After we ate, we sat around, talked, listened to albums by Red Fox and other comics, and then we played board games.

We even went to the drive-in movie, which was different from what we were used to in Dillon—it was integrated. We did not experience any discrimination while we were there. The only problem I had was finding a straightening comb.

We had only been in Colorado for a few months when we decided to drive back to Dillon for Thanksgiving. I did see Lennie but only because Mrs. Nora insisted. Lennie was her usual self, and the first thing she did was to remind me that I owed her money for the wedding.

We left shortly after Thanksgiving, and we were on our way back to Colorado. On our way back, we lost a hubcap, and it was cold and snowing. Chris was use to driving in the snow because he lived and went to school in Washington, D.C. He was determined to find that hubcap, so he stopped the car beside the road and walked back down the highway. He returned with that hubcap.

We finally made it back to Colorado. After we settled in, we started our daily routines. I was working, and Chris was in school. I was learning to cook some, but not very well.

During the Christmas holidays, Mrs. Nora decided to come visit us. She had two weeks off for Christmas. Mrs. Nora taught school, so she decided to use part of her break to come to Colorado. This was her first time flying, and her first time in Colorado.

We had planned to take her to see many interesting things while she was there. We took her to see the city, which was very pretty in December because of the Christmas lights and decorations.

I should have let Mrs. Nora cook dinner at least once while she was there, but I was trying to impress her. This sure did not help with our appetites. I was not a cook, although you would have thought I would be since I grew up in a restaurant, but Lennie did not have time to teach me and she always said I was in the way. I did learn to fry fish, pork chops, and chicken. However, I could not cook anything else. Chris's mother did not teach him how to cook or do anything domestic, either. We were pitiful—the blind leading the blind.

We sat down and ate the dinner I prepared. I cooked fried chicken, sweet peas, and rice, and we had brown dinner rolls and Hi-C. This was not bad for someone who could not cook.

Mrs. Nora's vacation with us was over; we took her to the airport for her flight back to South Carolina. We enjoyed her visit and hated to see her leave.

Chris's classes were almost over, and we were anxious to find out where we were going from there. My job with IBM was almost over; however, some of us were offered permanent jobs with the IBM Company in Colorado Springs. Because we were here temporarily, I couldn't accept a permanent job; it sure would have been nice—the pay was good and the opportunity was excellent.

To celebrate the closing of the school session for Chris and the others who were there, a banquet was given in honor of the students and their spouses and companions. There was a nice formal sit-down dinner, with tables that were set with the best china, crystal, and silverware. We had cocktail hour before dinner and did a lot of socializing. During a conversation with other wives and classmates of Chris, I made a comment about the food, not realizing that I split a verb. Chris immediately corrected me in front of everyone, saying "You used the wrong verb!" I felt like a dummy. Of course, he told me which verb I was supposed to use, "It's edible, not eatable!"

Everyone was quiet for a moment, and then someone spoke up and said, "Everyone take your seats, and let's get ready for dinner." For the first time in my life, I was totally embarrassed and wanted to run away and hide; but I took my seat next to my husband and tried to enjoy my dinner. Did Chris apologize to me? No, why should he—he didn't do anything wrong, I did.

I became very self-conscience about holding conversations with other people after the ordeal with Chris at the banquet. When I attended affairs after that, I didn't have confidence in what I said; therefore, I kept my mouth shut, and from this I developed a sense of insecurity about myself.

Some of the students wanted to stay at Lowery as instructors for the school. We finally got our orders, and we were going to

Florida, to Eglin Air Force Base. This time, we let the military pack up our belongings and had them shipped to Florida.

In the meantime, I found out I was pregnant with our daughter. When we got to Dillon, we told family and friends that they were going to be grandparents, aunts, and uncles for the first time on both sides of the family—at least, that's what we thought.

OUR TOUR AT EGLIN AIR FORCE BASE, FLORIDA 1967

Before we left Colorado, Chris's commanding officer asked him during out-processing if he would have a problem living on the base in a southern state like Florida, since he was in an interracial marriage. Chris told him that he was not in an interracial marriage and that his wife was black. The officer looked at the picture on my ID card and assumed I was white.

I grew up in the black environment, so this was what I had known since I was about nine years old. I did not think about the difference; I guess because being black had become part of my life, and I did not have thoughts of being anyone else.

After we arrived in Florida, we found a place to stay while Chris processed in. We found a nice, furnished apartment with one bedroom because we would be moving on the base as soon as housing was available.

We enjoyed the beach and met other people there who were military and civilians. We met a few couples who were also alumni from the same school as Chris.

Chris liked watching football games, so one night we were sitting on the sofa, and I was teasing him as I always did. This particular time, I tickled him, and he told me to stop, but I continued. Then, he told me again to stop, but this time, he slapped me across my face. I was shocked that he hit me like that; he had never hit me before. Once again, he didn't say, "I 'm sorry." He just continued to watch the football game as though nothing had happened. Of course, I left him alone. I thought that maybe I asked for it.

After a few months, we had base housing. We continued to meet people, and we went to each other's homes and had coffee, or they played cards and exchanged stories about places they had been. I went to luncheons and card parties with other officers' wives.

We started buying things for the baby: a crib, baby clothes and Birdseye clothe diapers (disposable weren't that popular), sheets, a mobile for the crib, and all the little things you need for a baby. Because they didn't have the technology to tell you if you were having a boy or girl, we had to wait until the birth; therefore, we bought things that were of neutral colors. We bought baby bottles (a Playtex nurses set) the one with the bags for the bottles; we did know that we would be using formula. Breastfeeding was not very popular, and no one impressed upon us to do so.

I started doing ceramics with some of the other wives on the base, and I learned how to make a lot of nice things. I actually enjoyed the hobby.

We got a letter from Mrs. Nora and Chris's sister Angela telling us that they were coming to visit with us for awhile. We were excited and looked forward to them coming. We prepared the guest room we had and did some grocery shopping. I knew they would enjoy doing ceramics and shopping.

They drove to Florida, and when they arrived, we met them at the gate because we lived on the base, and you had to have a visitor's pass to get on. We were so glad to see them; I know Chris was. We talked and laughed, and they told us about the things that they experienced on their trip.

After a good night's sleep, we had breakfast and took them on a tour around the base, and then we went shopping. We had a great time doing ceramics, and we found a place where we could buy fresh vegetables, and, thank goodness, they cooked all kinds of good meals for us. Of course, I learned a little bit more about cooking; I was getting better.

Before Chris's family got there, we had looked for and bought a dinette set, living room furniture, and a bedroom suit.

When we were in Colorado, I had problems finding ethnic products, and that's when I started using a perm in my hair, which worked out great. During one of our trips to Pensacola, Chris and I found a shop that had ethnic products. I was able to get hair oil and other products that we needed but could not find on the base. Chris's family enjoyed shopping and sightseeing.

Mrs. Nora and Angela stayed almost two weeks with us before they had to leave. They started getting all the things that they were going to take with them, and we helped them pack the car. We really hated to see them leave; we had so much fun talking, laughing, and cooking. We missed them.

One morning, I was doing the laundry, and, in the process of transferring the clothes from the washer to the dryer, I found condoms in the bottom of the washer. "What in the world is this doing in here," I asked myself. I was standing there, pregnant, and wondering why Chris needed condoms. I placed them on the dresser in the bedroom, and when Chris came home from work, I told him I found condoms in the wash with his shirts.

We were sitting on the bed in the bedroom, and he started crying. He said, "I never thought I would lie to my wife!" He began to explain about one of the girls with whom we all hung out, who was single, very nice, and a civilian worker. He said he approached her, and she turned him down. He said, "She told me that she had too much respect for you to sleep with me." Chris didn't have an affair with the woman even though that was his intention, but she turned him down. That was the first time the infidelity started; I forgave him, and I didn't bring it up anymore.

On October 13, 1967, our daughter, Nicole, was born. This was a beautiful little seven-pound, twenty-one inch-long baby girl, with a head full of hair that was straight, with a light brown tint on the ends.

The nurse came in my room at the hospital for me to sign the birth certificate. After looking over the information that was on the document, I noticed the letter "C" where race was indicated and asked the nurse what it stood for. She told me Caucasian. I told her Nicole's race was black; however, she did look like a little white baby. In the sixties, blacks were referred to as blacks, which should have been a "B." Anyway, the nurse changed the race to what it was supposed to be.

October 13 was an important date to Chris and his family because that was the date that his father died.

CHRIS'S OVERSEAS TOUR TO THAILAND 1967 TO 1968

Chris finally received orders sending him overseas for a year. We decided to put our furniture in storage and move Nicole and me to Dillon. We would stay there with his family during his tour overseas.

Chris finished processing out, and we packed the car and drove to Dillon with our little bundle of joy, whom everyone was anxious to see.

After arriving in Dillon, Chris's family was excited to see Nicole. We settled in and visited friends the next day; of course, we had to show our baby off. Chris's stay was not long because he had to leave for Colorado to attend school for six weeks.

That was a long six weeks that Chris was gone. He called, and he always wanted to know what Nicole was doing. Chris had a concern about Nicole's skin color; he always asked if she had gotten darker.

Luckily, I was rehired at the same school in which I worked when Chris and I got married. However, I was going to need a babysitter for Nicole. The mother of a friend of Mrs. Nora's agreed to keep her, and she did a great job. She had a lot of old folks' remedies—for example, when Nicole had the hiccups, she put a toothpick in her hair to stop them.

After awhile, we found another woman who could come to the house to keep my daughter; she would also house clean. When she came the first week, we really liked her; she cleaned the kitchen to the point where we didn't recognize it anymore. Nicole was clean and fed. So we decided to keep her, and that worked out for awhile. Then, sometimes, on Monday mornings, she did not show up; we decided to let her go, and I ended up staying home with my daughter.

Mrs. Nora and Angela decided to build an addition to their house. They needed more room, including a larger kitchen and another bathroom.

Angela was a music major, and she needed a special place to teach piano lessons and store her music; she also played for the church.

During the summer with Angela, Mrs. Nora, and Elfie out of school Angela and I decided to drive to Washington DC to visit Aunt Rosa.

Angela and Aunt Rosa had a passion for eating crabs. So we would drive to the wharf where they would buy a case of live blue crabs. It was an experience watching them put those live crabs into a pot of boiling water mixed with Obay Seafood Seasoning, beer, and some other stuff to steam them. Nicole was so excited, she would scream, laugh, and point to the crabs so that her aunt Angela would get them; she watched the crabs scrambling around and trying to get out of the pot.

When we arrived in Washington, D.C., Nicole was about eight months old, and she wasn't walking. We were staying with Aunt Rosa, however, and her apartment was very small; in fact, there was only one bedroom, and there was very little crawling space for Nicole. We had to carry her around most of the time. One day, Nicole decided that enough was enough, and she started taking steps slowly. Then she realized that she could get around better, so she started walking.

Angela and I returned to Dillon from our visit with Aunt Rosa. We bought extra crabs and packed them on ice so Angela could cook them for Mrs. Nora and Elfie. Mrs. Nora was excited that Nicole was walking and actually running.

Thanksgiving and Christmas would soon arrive, and I was helping Mrs. Nora, Angela, and Elfie shop and decorate the house. Plus, they were getting ready for the Annual Christmas dance.

Chris wrote to tell me he was coming home for the holidays. Of course, we were excited. This would also be Nicole's first Christmas.

Angela and Mrs. Nora told me that Noah, Angela's son, was coming to visit for Christmas; he would only be here for a few days. Chris, didn't know about Noah, so we were going to tell him that this was a young man we were giving Christmas to. Chris didn't know that his sister Angela had a son, who was then twelve years old. Noah was physically challenged and had some deformities when he was born and was placed in a facility where he could get professional help.

Noah was supposed to stay for a few days, but for some reason, he was in the kitchen and placed a dishcloth on one of the eyes on the stove and it caught fire. This wasn't life—threatening, but

Mrs. Nora and Angela felt Noah wasn't ready to be around people, so they took him back to the facility where he lived. Chris did ask who Noah was, and I told them someone with whom his mom and sister wanted to spend Christmas. Mrs. Nora was a very private person and she didn't want Chris or anyone to see the imperfections in her family; therefore, she tried to cover them up.

We had a wonderful Christmas, watching Nicole enjoy her toys and exchanging gifts. We also had a great family dinner, and, of course, we were glad Chris was with Nicole for her first Christmas.

The end of January, Mother Emma passed. Lennie had the funeral at the Baptist Church, where Mother Emma was a member for many years. I knew I would miss her because she was the grandmother I really didn't have in my life after leaving my biological family.

Chris's leave was up, and he went back overseas to complete his tour. In a few weeks, I received a letter from Chris telling me we were going back to Florida; he sent copies of his orders so that I could make arrangement to have household goods picked up and get things ready for his return home.

I took Nicole and Fran with me to Myrtle Beach Air Force base to get a set of American Tourister luggage that Chris told me to purchase. Chris would be coming back to South Carolina, and from there, we were moving back to Florida.

OUR RETURN TO EGLIN AIR FORCE BASE 1968

The movers came and picked up our household goods, and Chris was on his way home.

Chris was home for a few days, and we had to say our goodbyes to everyone. At least Mrs. Nora, Angela, Elfie, and Lennie got a chance to spend the first year of Nicole's life with her.

We packed the car and left for Florida the next morning. We drove all day and arrived on the base for Chris to process-in. We found a nice apartment until quarters were available on the base.

We took Nicole to the beach, where she enjoyed playing in the water. We met a lot of people and began to settle in. Soon, we received quarters and had our household goods moved on base.

I decided to register for a keypunch course after we were settled in. When I worked for IBM in Colorado, I was fascinated with keypunch and wanted to learn the skill. I went at night to a local community college, and Chris watched Nicole. I completed the course and received my certificate.

We met a couple who lived down the street from us, Terri and Winston, a couple from North Carolina with whom we spent a lot of time. Terri and I went shopping at the Base Exchange and sat and talked. Our tours were up about the same time when she found out she was pregnant with their first child. We kept in touch for awhile after we left, and then we went in different directions.

Before our tour was up, Chris decided to apply for AFIT a program through the military; in this program, they send you to school to get your Master's degree. Chris would go to Wright Patterson in New Jersey, if accepted. He said, "If I am accepted, we will stay in the military; if not, my commitment will be up and we'll become civilians."

He was not accepted into AFIT, and he started putting in resumes to different companies. We went on interviews in South Carolina and North Carolina. We wanted to be close to family, particularly Chris's family; this man was devoted to his mother. I had heard people say that a man who is dedicated to his mother will make a good husband.

Chris was offered jobs with most of the companies where he interviewed, and finally, he accepted the one in Fayetteville, North Carolina. This job would also put us closer to Dillon, where family was.

OUR MOVE TO
FAYETTEVILLE 1970

After we processed out of the military and traveled to Fayetteville, we stayed with his family for a few days. We were looking for a house to buy in Fayetteville, which would be our first home.

We found a four-bedroom house that was in a good subdivision; it was growing, and it would be great for Nicole and any other children we might have. There was a nice backyard for her to play in, and we didn't have to worry about traffic since it was on a cul-de-sac.

We bought the house and began to settle in. Each weekend, however, we went to Dillon and to church. We visited with friends, and after Sunday dinner, we sat around and talked, then it was time for us to return to Fayetteville. I would take Nicole to see Lennie and her husband while we were there.

After awhile, we stopped going every weekend. We had been in Fayetteville about a year when we had this thunderstorm and lightening struck the house. I was in the kitchen cooking and had no idea that the house on the opposite end was burning. A gentleman came to the carport door, and when I went to see what he wanted, he told me there was a hole in the roof on the opposite end of the house, and it was on fire. I was starting down the hall and saw the smoke. I remember telling Nicole to put up her toys and put them in her toy box, which was in her room. And for some reason she wouldn't; I guess that was why.

Neighbors called the fire department and helped me get clothes out of the house. We put them in the car. This was on a Thursday, because I always had the car on that day to run errands and grocery shop. Chris carpooled with one of his co-workers. One of my neighbors came over and took Nicole home with her; she lived across the street, and Nicole was familiar with her and her family.

Chris came home shortly after the fire department arrived. There was no way to warn Chris about the house being on fire because he was on his way home, and we didn't have cell phones then. He was carpooling and found out when he turned the corner to the street we lived on. When he got there and saw that this was his house that was burning, he was devastated. He started helping us get things out of the house and made sure we were alright.

The fire did some serious damage, and we were not able to stay in the house. We cut everything off, closed everything we could, and drove to Dillon. We didn't worry about anything in the house because people were different then. You could leave your windows and doors open, and you were safe. We spent the night in Dillon at Mrs. Nora's. We explained to them what had happened and returned to Fayetteville the next morning.

We contacted the insurance company, and they told us to move into an apartment that was a few blocks from our house. We were to live there until the house could be repaired, and our furniture was placed in storage.

Now Lennie had never been to our house, even though we had been there for over a year. She called us and said, "We are coming up there to visit for awhile." This was on a Sunday afternoon. We told her fine; we were surprised because she had never expressed the desire to come before. A couple who were friends of theirs and Mrs. Nora brought them to Fayetteville.

After they got here, Lennie went inside of the burned house and told me not to put glory into material things because something will happen to it. She looked around and said her granddaughter needed a fenced in backyard so she wouldn't have to worry about anything or anyone bothering her.

Lennie had been sick; I didn't know what was wrong with her but I knew something was because she had lost a lot of weight. This started happening before she came to Fayetteville to visit us. They spent most of the afternoon with us, and she had a chance to spend time with Nicole. After they left I still couldn't believe that she came.

Shortly after her trip to Fayetteville, I was called and told to come to Dillon because she was in the hospital. When we got there that evening, visiting hours at the hospital were over.

We went to Mrs. Nora's and settled in for the night. I left Nicole with Chris and his family so I could go back to the hospital that morning. When I got to the hospital that morning, her friend Margie was there with her; her husband had gone home. Lennie was not alert, and she passed shortly after I got there. I stood there and watched her die. This was an experience I would not want to witness again. I asked the nurse what the cause of death was, and she told me Lennie had stomach cancer. At that moment, I don't know what I felt; I didn't cry. I was sad, but I felt empty. This woman who had been in my life since I was eight years old was gone, and there was no more Lennie; I could no longer wonder how she really felt about me, because she never expressed it verbally or emotionally. Now, she couldn't.

When I was ready to leave the hospital, they gave me a paper bag with her belongings in it, and I thought, *This is all that's left of her, what's in this bag.*

I helped her husband make the arrangements for her funeral. I still don't understand why she treated me the way she did. The funeral went well; she had written on a piece of paper that we found in the nightstand beside her bed what funeral home she wanted to have her body, but her husband had already given her to another one. She also wrote who she wanted to eulogize her funeral, and we were able to fulfill that wish. After the funeral, I knew that I would have to check on her husband to make sure he was alright.

We returned to Fayetteville and we still had to oversee the completion of the repairs to the house. We fulfilled Lennie's wish to install the redwood privacy fence she wanted for Nicole. We finally moved back into the house before Christmas, but we spent the holiday in Dillon.

A family from Dillon who was very close to Lennie's husband and Mrs. Nora told us about a young lady who was coming to Fayetteville on weekends to spend with her husband; he worked here.

Ashley called us one Saturday evening and told us who she was and said that they wanted to meet us. She and her husband Barry came by that Sunday on their way back to South Carolina. They only stayed for a short while, just long enough for us to get acquainted and make sure we had each other's phone numbers. We had a good visit and found out that they had a son who was about the same age as Nicole.

As soon as school was out for the summer, she was moving to Fayetteville with their son, Jeremiah. After she moved here and got settled, we spent a lot of time together. We did our shopping together on that designated day, Thursday, and cooked and had dinner together. The guys watched football.

They were here for maybe a year, and then Barry was transferred to Greensboro. I really hated to see them leave because Ashley was like a sister to me; she still is. After they were settled in Greensboro, Ashley called to tell me she was pregnant with their daughter. We continue to communicate and keep up with what is going on with our families. We don't see each other as often as we would like, but we get together whenever we can.

I was pregnant with our son, Brice, who was born on January 13, 1972; Nicole and Brice were both born on the thirteenth, although they are four years apart. Brice weighed eight pounds, eleven-and-a-half ounces, and he was twenty-one inches long.

Brice was about two months old when I received a call from my mama telling us that she and two of my brothers were coming to see us. This was my younger brother who had just returned from Vietnam. He had written me and sent pictures while he was there. He wanted to see me and tell me he was getting married and he was bringing his fiancé. When I told Chris they were coming he said, "If anyone else comes by the house while they are here, you need to tell them that these are friends of yours; don't tell them that they are your family." He didn't want anyone to know that my family was white.

The sad thing was a few weeks after their visit; my brother was killed in a car accident a few miles from mamas' house. Returning to my mama's house for the funeral was the first time since becoming an adult. The house was as I remembered it from a little girl. My brother's body lay in state in the living room, which was customary. However, I had never seen this before. In the meantime, I was talking with my eldest brother. I asked him, "Where is our stepfather?" I was looking for a tall, slender man, the one I remembered as a little girl who appeared to be tall.

My brother said, "He is standing over there." I looked and sure enough that was him, a short, slim man. I didn't believe my eyes. I was looking for the tall man that stood over me and tried to get me to do that horrible act on him. I didn't say anything to him; there was nothing to say.

After the funeral, we returned home and Mama wrote to let me know what was going on with everyone.

Mrs. Nora was the type of person who always reached out to help someone. One night she called and said, "I have this young lady who needs somewhere to stay, and I thought bringing her to Fayetteville to stay with you all would be a safe place for her to be right now." Hannah was eighteen, and Mrs. Nora knew that her family wouldn't have a clue that she would be with us. We agreed and told her that it was alright to bring her.

She lived with us for almost a year, and then she moved in with a lady whom she had met and who had a two-bedroom apartment. I don't think this lasted too long before she met Marie, who lived in an apartment in the same complex.

Hannah and Marie became best of friends and shared the apartment for a long time. Then Marie decided to move to

New York. A few months later, Hannah moved to New York with Marie and stayed there until she decided to go into the military. After her basic training, Hannah received orders to go to Japan for fourteen months.

She would write often to let us know how she was doing. During Hannah's tour, she met a guy and told us she was pregnant. Her tour was up, and Hannah had orders to San Antonio, Texas, which is where she had Malinda.

After Malinda was born, Hannah and her friend, Henri, came to Fayetteville with the baby. Hannah had put in for a change in duty stations and was in transition to Colorado, where Henri was stationed. She wanted us to keep Malinda until she was settled. We actually kept her from July to September.

Hannah did really well in the military and eventually retired in Charleston before moving to Charlotte, North Carolina. In 2007, Hannah died from a heart condition. We will always cherish the time we had with her.

Her daughter, Malinda, has a son who is six years old, and they live in Charlotte. Hannah only had the one daughter. The death of Malinda's mother has been extremely hard on her. She is and always will be part of this family.

THE INFIDELITY AND SEPARATION

Chris and I had established our roots in Fayetteville and had been married for nine years. He worked for the same company for a few years. Then one day he came home from work and told me he wanted to ask me a serious question. He asked me if I had been seeing anyone.

"What are you talking about?" I asked. "How could I, when I was always focused on you?" I couldn't believe what I was hearing.

The reason he asked was because he was being treated for an STD that he had gotten from one of his women. I was so mad that I actually started laughing; I guess because I was in shock.

I found out that the two women with whom he had had affairs worked at the plant, and both of them were military wives with husbands overseas. I actually talked with both of them. One was very apologetic and told me Chris was very persistent and that she gave in and met with him at a motel. The other one didn't live too far from our subdivision, and her first name was the same as mine.

She told me in a phone conversation, "I love Chris, and I want to have his baby; you have the cutest little boy," she said. "I told Chris he didn't get STD from me; he needed to ask you." I could have really hurt that woman, but she wasn't worth it. Chris had some nerve to take our son with him to meet this woman; he must have been desperate. So I confronted Chris with all that I had learned. Chris admitted having the affairs, but he didn't say he was sorry. I was through talking with the women. I continued to deal with the infidelity and pretended that everything was okay.

We were going to Dillon almost every weekend to spend time with family and friends. We would arrive in Dillon on a Friday evening, and as soon as we pulled the car into the driveway and before we could get the kids and our bags out of the car, Chris went across the street to see Beverly. Her mother wasn't home; she was at work. Because Chris had known Beverly and her family for years, he knew he could go over there anytime that he wanted, and it would be okay.

Each time, Mrs. Nora would be cooking dinner for us, and when she was ready to put the food on the table, she would ask, "Where is Chris?" When Angela told her that he was across the street, Mrs. Nora would go over there and get him.

Chris went over there every time we went to Dillon. One night, I actually dreamed that he was sleeping with this young lady. She was at least twelve years younger than Chris; plus, Chris had a wife and children. One day I said to Chris, "You know, I had a dream that you were having an affair with Beverly when we went to Dillon. Is this true?"

"Yes," he said, "I was." He didn't lie about these women when I confronted him; he would admit it, but he never said, "I am sorry."

Chris and I had been married for nine years, and this wasn't the first time he cheated. He cheated the first year we were married when I was pregnant with our daughter. He never realized how much his infidelity could hurt. His attitude was "yes, I did it, and that's that."

I thought that I was the reason he was cheating. I thought I wasn't smart enough, that maybe I didn't look good enough—all kinds of things went through my mind. I wanted answers, and there were none.

When I married Chris, I had no idea that he would turn out to be this kind of husband or person. I knew he was moody and controlling, but I did not know that he was a womanizer. I didn't think he had it in him. I began to wonder if it was something I didn't do or could have done better.

Chris's cheating haven was through a friend and co-worker. He used his friend's apartment to meet with one of his women, the one who had the same name as mine. His friend came to our house and sat with me while I was cooking dinner and doing other household chores for my husband and family.

After all this, I still tried to make my marriage work. I wanted to show him that I was a better woman than those other women were. I changed my appearance by cutting my hair; I bought clothes instead of making them. I could not believe that this man had the knowledge to know how to cheat. I thought he was too much of a nerd.

Nothing seemed to work. I didn't think this was the way my marriage would end. I confided in Mrs. Nora about her son and his infidelity. This is the man I married, but this was her son, and she was very protective of him, no matter how wrong he was. I was supposed to ignore Chris's behavior and be the accepting, forgiving wife; I had to deal with it and let bygones be bygones. Mrs. Nora's response was, "Oh shucks, honey, he is only sowing his wild oats. Get over it. This happens all the time, and you need to look the other way."

After I saw where Mrs. Nora was going with that, I realized I had confided in the wrong person. No matter what Chris had done, as far as she was concerned, it was acceptable.

Now was the time to start a life for me and the kids. First, I had to find a job. With outdated skills and no experience, I had no idea where to start. I had not worked in eight years, and I didn't have a college degree, and I had no money.

I had no savings; there was nothing. I depended on Chris for everything. I never thought my marriage would end up in a courtroom, with no family to help me get through what was inevitable.

Thank God I had good friends. I trusted the man I married, and thought he loved me, and I thought I loved him. At that point, though, it wasn't about love, it was about survival.

I set aside my life to make sure his life was fulfilled. I made my own clothes and did all the work around the house, including cutting the grass. I took care of and raised wonderful children. But this is what I was supposed to do—don't get me wrong, I enjoyed being home with our kids.

When we moved to Fayetteville I had the opportunity to get a civil service job as a keypunch operator. I completed the training and had my certificate. Chris told me the little money I would make would be just enough for daycare, and it would not be worth me going to work. Plus, he didn't want to be dependent on his wife's income. He felt that he could support his family with his income only.

So, I listened to him. I stayed home and became a true-to-heart housewife. I did whatever I could do to make it easy for Chris on the weekends and economize with the food by canning and freezing vegetables, and sometimes fruit, to stock the pantry so that we would have more money.

I tried to deal with Chris's infidelity, but I couldn't. I told him, "Look, you need to move out; this isn't working." I was too hurt and couldn't stand to look at him. He finally moved in with his friend. I decided to file for a legal separation through the courts. We went to court, and Chris had to pay child support, and he had visitation rights to see the kids. He was ordered to pay the house mortgage, as well. We were separated for almost two years.

I guess Mrs. Nora thought I was going to attack her son or something because she always drove from Dillon to Fayetteville to be with him when he picked the kids up for his visitation, which was not overnight.

On one of his visits to pick up the kids, we were arguing about him leaving cotton balls and fish food on the steps for the gold fish, when I really need clothes and food for his children.

We were in the bedroom when I told him about the stupid gold fish, and he didn't like what I said as usual; therefore, he grabbed me by my arm and pinned me down on the bed. He straddled me and hit me in my face with his fist. In the meantime, his legs were spread and something told me to attack his jewels. When I did this he was up and out the door, bent over. I guess I hurt him.

When the one person I thought would always be there for me "in sickness and health, for better or worse, for richer or poorer, until death do you part," decided to ignore those promises and leave, I had to do the best I could, which was heartbreaking. I believed Chris would always be there and that he would try to make his marriage work. But I was living in a fantasy world.

This is when I realized that even as a housewife, I should have continued to take classes to update my skills for employment. Chris told me I didn't have to worry about anything because he would make sure I was taken care of. Of course I believed him.

My skills were so outdated; I was ashamed to even apply for secretarial jobs. It took this experience for me to wake up and smell the coffee, so to speak. I realized that I should always take care of myself no matter what someone promised me. Even though I didn't work, I should have kept my skills updated by taking classes or even working part time.

When I went by my adopted dad's house in Dillon and asked him for help, at least until I could get a job, he told me, "I don't want to get involved, and you do what you can."

I left my adopted dad and Mrs. Trudy's and went to my friend Morgan's house. Her mother, Mrs. Houston, knew what I was going through and gave me food from her freezer to take home. I returned to Fayetteville, knowing that I had to grow up and take care of my kids.

I had gained confidence in myself and was learning how to budget and feed my kids. I got a job in downtown Fayetteville, working part time from nine in the morning to one in the afternoon, as a secretary/bookkeeper. This worked well because I was at home when the kids went to school, and I was there when they got out of school.

I was a member of a local Baptist Church and sang in the gospel choir. One Sunday evening, Mrs. Harris and I had gone with the gospel choir to a singing engagement, when my left side started bothering me. It felt like there was a catch was in my lower back, and it hurt to walk.

After getting home and dropping Mrs. Harris off, who lived next door to me, I got the kids settled down for the night because they had school the next day and I had to go to work. I had had this problem with my hip before, and usually the pain would be gone by morning. It didn't go away this time, and the next morning I could hardly get out of bed. I literally had to crawl on the floor because the pain was so bad I could hardly stand up. I called Nicole and told her to call Mrs. Harris, who was not only my neighbor but like a second mother to me. I had Nicole ask her if she could come to the house.

Mrs. Harris came over and asked what was wrong. I asked if she would help the kids get ready for school, and she did. I was in a carpool with a few other parents, and, luckily, it was their time to drive the kids to school. After the kids left for school, I asked Mrs. Harris to take me to the doctor. After we got to the doctor's office and explained to him what was going on, he gave me a shot in my hip to help the pain subside. I did feel better for awhile but that didn't correct the problem. Little did I know that this would be an on going problem for me.

I went back to the doctor because the problem was still there; he sent me to see an orthopedic doctor. After having x-rays done I was told that I had scoliosis (a curved spine), which was not good. He put me on ten days of bed rest and gave me medication to relax the muscles around my spine.

I did as I was told, and Mrs. Harris and her cousin Sam took care of me and my kids. I was able to walk around, but the pain was bad. After the bed rest, I went back to see the doctor to find out that he wanted to put me in the hospital for ten days. This hospitalization would include physical therapy. I had no choice at the time. Mrs. Harris and Sam kept my kids at their house and continued to help me with my situation.

Before I was released from the hospital, Chris called my room and told me, "You might as well leave the hospital because I am not paying for you to stay there!" My doctor came in the room just as I was hanging up the phone, and he noticed that I was upset and crying, so he asked me what was wrong. I began telling him what Chris said. The doctor told me not to concern myself with what Chris said but to concentrate on what I needed to do to get better. Maybe two or three days later, Chris came by the hospital to see me and told me, "You don't have to worry about the hospital bill; stay as long as you need to. I'll take care of everything." I learned later that the company Chris worked for was being sold, and he would possibly be out of a job.

When I was released from the hospital, Mrs. Harris told me I would have to come back to their house to stay with them, so I went home with Mrs. Harris and Sam, and I stayed with them for awhile. Chris, Mrs. Nora, and Elfie came by to see the kids, and they started talking about taking them to South Carolina with them. Mrs. Harris told them, "There is no way you are going to take these kids from this house; that will never happen. If you want to do something, you can buy these kids some clothes." Mrs. Nora, I guess, thought that they had what they needed. She left and came back with clothes. After Mrs. Harris talked with

Mrs. Nora, I believe she understood that she wasn't in charge in that house.

I continued to stay with Mrs. Harris for awhile longer, but had to go back in the hospital for more tests and therapy. This time, Chris told me he would be without a job and I had lost my job. I had a conversation with Nicole's godmother, who said to me, "Chris is the father of those kids; let him take care of them. Let him come back home, and remember that you can live with anyone, if you put your mind to it; you could do worse." I thought about it and realized at that time she was right, so I decided to let Chris come back home and hoped that maybe he would be a different person.

After we were settled back at home, Chris and I made some decisions. He was hired by the company that bought-out the one he worked for. I continued to recuperate and decided to go back to school. Because I was impulsive, school didn't work out for me at the time. Instead, I started volunteering at the school that our children were in, and eventually I started substitute-teaching.

I was determined to either finish school or get a job or both; I wasn't going to have that same experience again. Besides, who was to say if I could really trust Chris anyway?

I think this is why some marriages struggle; because the trust isn't there any more. Women and some men guard their hearts, not knowing if the person will stray again or decide to be the master of his soul by learning to appreciate what he chose from the beginning.

I have a quiet personality, and I am easily intimidated, not just by Chris but those that I chose to be friends with. It is hard for me to say no, and I have difficulty expressing what I really feel; I give in too easily. When some people see the weaknesses in a person, I believe they take advantage.

I allowed Chris and some of my friends to take advantage of my weaknesses because I didn't want them to be mad at me. He and others used the weaknesses to gain control over me. In allowing this to happen, my self-esteem and self confidence were both lowered. Of course, my self-esteem was lower when I lived with my adopted mother.

If I had an opinion, I would not express it because I thought—based on what the other person had to say—that I would be wrong or my opinion wasn't important. I was agreeable even though I didn't agree. I had this desire to please others in order to be liked. When you do this, you are not pleasing yourself, and you are not a whole person.

We went on family vacations during the summer months; the vacations were planned by Chris, and the kids enjoyed themselves. The kids were getting older and participating in school and community activities, which meant we didn't go out of town as much.

As the years went by, I accepted a job as a teacher's assistant and worked for a year and a half. The problems with my back continued, and I was often in traction and on muscle relaxers. I had a lot of pain in my lower back, which affected my walking at times.

Chris was becoming the person he always was, and I knew he had a controlling spirit, just as Lennie had, which I learned to deal with. Their personalities were very similar; I guess that's why I lived with it. I didn't know any better.

For some reason, I was afraid to let go. When Lennie gave me reason to leave, I did, but I soon returned for whatever reason. Chris treated me like dirt, and, even though he left, I still allowed him to return, hoping he would change. I knew what these two people were all about, but I continued to hang on to them.

We were in Dillon one weekend, and I met Mary Alice and her husband Harold. Mary Alice reminded me of Lennie. She said, "You don't remember me, but I am your godmother." She told me that she and Harold had retired and moved to Fayetteville from New York. I asked her where they lived in Fayetteville and discovered that they lived within walking distance from us.

Mary Alice was short, with a small frame, and cute. She could have passed for white. She had straight, salt-and-pepper hair that reached her shoulders. She was a pleasant, likable person. She had a poodle named Penny that was almost human. She was trained to drink coffee out of a cup and saucer, and she even smoked a cigarette.

I enjoyed talking with Mary Alice because she told me how she and Lennie had been the best of friends for years. A few months later, Mary Alice and Harold decided to move to Bennettsville, South Carolina, where Harold's family lived.

On occasion, they came to visit with us. Harold was a carpenter and showed Chris how to do a lot of things like installing a pull-down attic door in the house for us.

Harold was tall about six—feet, two—inches tall and slim. He was a very nice man. We liked him. He worked in Fayetteville for awhile, and then he started doing odd jobs.

We visited with them on our way to Dillon and became attached to them. After I caught Chris with all those women, I talked with Mary Alice about it. She was disappointed in him, but Harold said he knew Chris had a problem and that he didn't treat me right.

There were friends of Chris's who were in Fayetteville and who had graduated from the same college. Chris wanted to invite them over to grill steaks. He asked me to make a salad and prepare baked potatoes. He went out and bought beer, and we had sodas.

I was in the den ironing clothes, and I knew I would finish well before the guests arrived. Chris asked me why I chose this time to iron when I knew company was coming. I told him that I would be through in a few minutes; I just needed to get it done. Chris was getting agitated, because he looked at me and said, "You need to put that away with your white a—self!" He never said anything like that to me before. I was shocked.

"What did you say?" I asked. He didn't answer me. I said, "I know you didn't said what I thought you said!" I went on to tell him that if that was how he felt, maybe I needed to put out the picture of my "white a—family" for his friends to enjoy. I said to Chris, "I wonder how my mama would feel knowing that you called her daughter a white a—." The funny thing is, he never referred to me that way before. Hearing him say this was a shocker to me!

He was upset because for the first time he didn't know if I would follow through on my words or not, so he wasn't taking any chances; he changed his plans. He called his friend and told him not to come because something had come up.

After things were back to normal for awhile, my stepmother, Mrs. Trudy, decided to show me her love by sending my high school pictures; they had been in the living room of the house I once lived in with Lennie and her husband. She also sent a note that read, "I am tired of looking at your ugly mug." I don't know where this came from or where she was going with this because I never called or bothered her for any reason. I didn't respond to what she did; I let it go.

Mrs. Trudy was determined to annoy me, so she wrote me a four-page letter on Holiday Inn stationery. The letter stated that she was tired of living in the run-down building (the business), and that I wasn't her husband's daughter, that he raised me. I don't remember everything she wrote—that was enough.

I took the letter and drove to Dillon. I stopped by my mother-in-law's and showed Mrs. Nora and Angela the letter, and they were surprised. Before reading the letter, they had often said that I was wrong to give my adopted dad a gift for Father's Day without giving Mrs. Trudy anything for Mother's Day. I tried to explain to them that Mrs. Trudy was not my mother, and I didn't feel as though I had to give her a gift when I didn't give my own biological mother a gift. I sent her a card each year, and I really didn't know her that well anyway.

Now they understood why I felt the way I did and agreed that she shouldn't have written that letter to me. I took the letter to my adopted dad so he could see what she had written. He read the letter, and I told him that she sent my high school pictures to me. He seemed surprised, and I told him she needed to leave me alone because I hadn't bothered her. He said, "I'll talk to her."

Before leaving Dillon, I decided to take the letter to the attorney that Lennie had used and explained to him what was going on. He told me that Lennie didn't have a will when she died and that I had inherited her share of the property that she and my adopted dad owned. This meant that my adopted dad and I had joint ownership of all the property that my stepmother thought belonged to him. He couldn't sell or borrow to make repairs or anything without my signature.

The attorney told me to wait in his office and that he would be right back. He went to the courthouse and obtained a copy of my adoption papers so there would not be any question about my legal rights. He also sent Mrs. Trudy a letter telling her if she continued to bother me, she would be charged with harassment. The attorney told me that the best thing that could happen would be for my stepmother to pack up her stuff and move back to where she came from.

Mrs. Trudy decided to buy her own house; that way, she didn't have to worry about me. They continued to run the business, and I am sure she made money, which was fine.

I didn't hear from her until one day she decided to try again by sending me a copy of the property taxes on the joint property in Dillon. She said, "You better pay these taxes, or he'll be in the street, because I'm not paying them." I ignored the papers and decided if that's the way she wanted it, that was fine. I had a place to live. I didn't hear anymore about taxes, so I guess they paid them.

After that, I didn't hear from her or from him until his mother died, and Mrs. Trudy called to let me know. If I had not known that I was adopted and where I came from, I would have been devastated by what Mrs. Trudy wrote in that letter she sent me. She wrote that I wasn't my adopted dad's daughter.

This is why parents should be open and honest with kids who have been adopted because they will find out. Unfortunately, someone else will tell them, some out of meanness, some plain out of ignorance. But it's better to tell them yourself. It may hurt, it may not; and sometimes, people are more understanding than we give them credit for being. However, information like that is always better coming from a parent than from a stranger.

My stepmother, Mrs. Trudy, probably assumed that I knew my adopted dad wasn't my father, but she still didn't have the right to tell me. I knew who my biological family was, and no one could tell me what I didn't already know.

My adopted mother, Lennie, tried to poison my mind and feelings for my family, but I knew who they were, and where they were, and why I was with her. I thank God for that.

As time passed, we continued to support our kids in school, and I continued working as a substitute teacher and taking care of my family.

Mrs. Nora became reacquainted with a guy she knew in the past. She brought him to visit us because he proposed to her, and she wanted our approval. She was very excited. Chris liked Mr. Stiles, and we thought he would be a good husband for Mrs. Nora. They had a lot in common; they liked to travel and enjoyed talking about community affairs. Angela had problems adjusting to her mother being married again, however.

Integration had taken place, and Angela lost her position as music and choir director. In the new high school, that position was given to the white music teacher from the white high school. The black high school was being transformed into an elementary school. A high school had been built for all Dillon students.

Angela could have taken a teaching position as a classroom history teacher, but she wasn't satisfied with that, and I don't blame her. Angela was hired to teach music, and she had a choir in another town in South Carolina, not far from Dillon. She was satisfied, and she was doing something she wanted to do—teaching music. With her church activities and school programs, she was happy.

After awhile, Angela decided to move to Fayetteville to live with us. She was always doing something to stay busy reading, and she enjoyed doing crafts. She finally got a job at Belk's as a salesperson, and she seemed to be content. She met a friend, and they were great together, but he didn't meet the approval of her mother or her brother.

During Angela's stay with us, their maternal grandmother died. This was a grandmother who was supposed to have died many years before but had been in a facility for many years.

Angela stayed with us for almost a year, and then she decided to return to Dillon. After awhile, we learned that she had cancer and was having treatments of chemotherapy and radiation. Angela was in a lot a pain, and, through it all, she lived for almost a year after her diagnosis.

After Angela's death, Mrs. Nora asked me if I would help her with the disposal of her daughter's things. I went to Dillon with my godmother, Mrs. Harris, a few months later to help Mrs. Nora go through Angela's things. She wanted to visit Noah while I was there, but the fact that Mrs. Harris was with me placed doubt in Mrs. Nora's' decision to visit Noah; she didn't want anyone to know about Noah being mentally challenged.

Mrs. Harris reassured her that she wasn't alone; these things happen in families, and no one is to blame, you have to accept the situation and go on. Mrs. Harris explained that she knew about Noah because Angela had told her when she was in Fayetteville. Mrs. Nora felt much better, and we went to see Noah. He always smiled, and he always knew his grandmother.

After our visit we went back to Dillon, and Mrs. Harris and I helped Mrs. Nora pack up her daughter's belongings.

I had a revelation from this experience: don't deny your family. This is what I had done most of my life, basically because I was told to. Things change, however, and now I don't have to anymore.

After Angela's death, we spent more time with Chris's mother and stepfather. In fact, we took them on vacations with us and did all the holidays with them in Dillon. The kids were older and really wanted to spend their holidays at home, but we made the sacrifice and went to Dillon. At this time, Mrs. Trudy had passed away, and we spent more time with my adopted dad, as well.

I continued to work as a substitute teacher, and later I was hired as a teacher's assistant in the same school that my son was attending. I worked for a year. Then the teacher I was working with asked me to do something she knew I wasn't good with, and she continued to insist that it be done. I finally told her to take her job and shove it. I left her classroom, went to the office, and told them I needed to leave for the day; I went home. The next day I returned to the school with a letter of resignation. I decided to enroll in Fayetteville State University to work on my degree, which I received a few years later. Thanks to that teacher, whom I learned a lot from.

Our daughter, Nicole, was in her last year of high school, and she was looking forward to going to college. Brice, our son, was in junior high school.

FAYETTEVILLE STATE UNIVERSITY GRADUATION 1984 TO 1987

I enrolled in Fayetteville State University and began the spring semester with one class, which was freshman math.

Chris wasn't optimistic about me going back to college; therefore, he was not as supportive as I thought he would be. He was so sure that I couldn't handle it, so he assumed I would quit.

I had already made up my mind that I was going to do what I had to do and graduate from college this time. I was determined to pay all my expenses for school, which I did by working as a substitute teacher on my days off from classes.

During my first year of study at Fayetteville State University, I received a North Carolina Incentive Grant for a year, which paid for my tuition. I didn't have to buy books during regular session because textbooks were rented. During the summer sessions, books had to be bought.

My advisor, Dr. Knight, had recommended me for a scholarship from Microsoft. She gave me the necessary information and told me to read up on Microsoft. I read through everything that was needed for the interview with the committee, which was in Raleigh, North Carolina.

I told Chris about the recommendation for a scholarship from Microsoft, and he wanted to know how it happened and who did this for me. He took me to Raleigh for the interview, which went well. The problem was that the scholarship was for a minority in a black college. My advisor assumed I was white, and, therefore, recommended me.

I believe Chris was intimated by anyone knowing about my biological family. He didn't want our friends to know that my family was white. That's why he didn't want my family visiting us when other friends of ours were coming by or were already there.

After successfully completing the required hours for a degree in Business Education, I got ready for graduation by celebrating with my family and a few friends with an evening out to dinner.

A dear friend of mine, Marla, whom I met during my enrollment at Fayetteville State University, was there, along with her family, Mr. and Mrs. Rogers, and Marla's brother, Tony; they had all come to attend her graduation.

MOVING INTO A DIFFERENT NEIGHBORHOOD 1987

Chris wanted to move into a more upscale neighborhood—that's what he called it. We had lived in our neighborhood for eighteen years; it was where our kids grew up.

Nicole graduated from high school and enrolled in college. She and her dad went house-hunting on one occasion, and they found a few that they liked. I had reservations about moving because I had lived in the one house for so long, and now I would have to start over again.

We found a house that was suitable for our family and in the same school district that Brice was already in. We didn't want to uproot him during his junior year in high school.

Just before Thanksgiving in 1987, as we were moving into the new house, the phone rang. It was Chris's mother calling to let us know that Elfie had passed. We were still in the process of moving and had to clean up the house we were moving from so the new tenants could move in.

I told Chris that he needed to go to Dillon to help his mother and that we would be there as soon as we finished getting things done. Chris left, and the kids and I finished moving and cleaning the other house.

The next day, we left for Dillon and arrived at Mrs. Nora's house. After saying our hellos to everyone, we went to the hotel where Chris had reserved a room for us. After the funeral, Chris stayed in Dillon to help Mrs. Nora with Elfie's estate. We returned to Fayetteville and continued to get the house in order.

Chris decided to buy Elfie's car and her house. After Chris received his and the kids' inheritance from Elfie, he made sure that I had nothing to do with any of their inheritance. He invested their money so only he would have access to it. He was eliminating me from anything that had to do with that money.

After receiving the inheritance, his attitude changed. His life had taken a turn financially; Chris was a lover of money. He felt as though he was the only person who had the knowledge to be successful. Mrs. Nora had always told him to associate with people who were successful and had prestige—in other words, rub elbows with the elite group of people.

His attitude was so bad that if you said anything to him, he snapped at you and made you feel like less than a person. Chris wasn't quite that bad before he inherited this money from Elfie.

The kids and I were concerned that he might have a stroke or something, so I approached Mrs. Nora once again about her son. I guess I will never learn. I told Mrs. Nora we had a concern about Chris's behavior and health. We didn't want him to have a heart attack or stroke because he was like a time bomb waiting to go off.

Once again, she defended her son. She said he was probably over-worked and that he was a good provider and that I should be grateful because I was a lucky girl to be living in a new house as nice as this one. Mrs. Nora pointed out that we need to be appreciative of all that Chris was doing for his family.

This was the last time I would approach my mother-in-law about her son. It didn't matter what he did from that time forward; I learned that in-laws are in-laws, and I wasn't going to set myself up again to be put in my place. I was only married to him; he was her son.

Shortly after I graduated from Fayetteville State, Chris decided to enroll in graduate school to get his Master's.

CHRIS'S GRADUATION FROM GRADUATE SCHOOL

Chris completed his studies and was getting ready to graduate. He told Mrs. Nora, and she and Mr. Stiles came up for his graduation.

Mrs. Nora was concerned about where Nicole should go to college. She and Chris didn't think she should go to the black historical schools; they believed she should go to the white Ivy League schools, which was fine, but the decision was basically Nicole's. I didn't say anything about what Mrs. Nora was doing until later.

Chris's graduation was on a Sunday morning, and Brice had been celebrating his prom the night before. Brice was a kid who was big for his age, and buying clothes for him was a challenge, so I bought sports coats and dress slacks or sweaters and nice dress shirts for him. This is what Brice wore to church and places where he had to dress up.

This particular day, we were sitting in the auditorium, and, of course, Mrs. Nora wanted to sit near the front, which we did. Brice and a family friend of ours, however, wanted to sit in the back. They had been out late because of the prom, and Brice wore a sweater and dress shirt with slacks, as did the other young man.

After the ceremony, we congratulated Chris, and we were getting ready to leave. Mrs. Nora was going to ride with Nicole and me, which was fine until she commented, "Everything was so nice, except Brice should have had on a suit." That, for me, was the straw that broke the camel's back; plus, a bad storm was coming up, and we needed to leave.

I told Mrs. Nora to sit up front with Nicole, who was driving, and I sat in the back. I started to tell Mrs. Nora so many things that I had previously held inside because I was taught to respect my elders. I spoke not out of disrespect to her, but to let her know that enough was enough. She had become critical of everything that was going on with my children. I told her that these were my kids, and I would appreciate it if she would stop telling us what she thought they should be doing. If she didn't like the way Brice was dressed, then she could buy him a suit or have her son Chris to buy him a suit. Chris was his father, and he lived with him, therefore, he knew what Brice had and didn't have."

This was not a pleasant conversation, but I had to tell her how I felt. Mrs. Nora took it personally, and after we arrived at our destination, which was a restaurant for dinner, she didn't want anything to do with me.

I told Chris what happened between his mom and me, and he told me she had spoken with him and that he told her that I have a tendency to overreact about things. I was on the bad list with them for a long time.

Nicole graduated from a predominately black college in North Carolina and had a job waiting for her in Charlotte, North Carolina.

She was going to live with our friends, Ashley and Barry, whom we met years before in Fayetteville.

Fran, from Dillon, was also living with us, and she and Nicole decided to go to the store to get some frozen yogurt.

When they left, I was going into the kitchen and I had to walk past Chris, who was standing near the steps. He grabbed me by my arm and said, "I am tired of you b----!" He pushed me on the sofa, which was in front of the double windows in the great room, not too far from where he was standing. He straddled me, had me pinned down, and he began to hit me in the face with his fist, repeatedly calling me a b----and a few other names. I remember him putting his knee in my throat and continuing to call me names and hitting me in the face. I thought I was going to die. I don't remember anything after that, except being on the floor. I heard my daughter say "What are you doing to my mother?"

I heard Chris reply, "We were talking!"

"That is not the way to talk!" she replied. Chris was kneeling over me wiping my face with a towel because there was blood on my mouth. I still don't remember how I ended up on the floor and I don't remember him getting a towel. Fran took Nicole out of the room, and I remember Chris leaving; he went into the bedroom. Nicole came back and asked me, "Mom, do you want to go to the hospital or what do you want to do?" I told her that I would be fine.

I didn't want to go to the hospital because I would have to explain what happened, and I didn't want to do that. I don't know why, maybe I was afraid Chris would be arrested and lose his job. I really don't know why I didn't do anything other than to tell him, "If you ever hit me or think of hitting me again, I will not hesitate to have you arrested and press charges against you!"

Shortly after that incident, Nicole left and moved to Charlotte to begin her new job. She said that she had to get out of the house and away from the situation; it was not a happy one. I understood what she meant, and I knew she had to go. Fran stayed around for a few months, and then she went back home and didn't return; she decided to help take care of an uncle who was not well.

I continued to deal with the situations in my marriage. One might ask why. I don't know. Maybe I was that insecure, maybe I was afraid that I couldn't make it on my own. I don't know; I don't have any answers. There are a lot of women in the same situation as mine who don't know what to do.

Chris never apologized; he never mentioned what he did or why he did it. No one would have believed that Chris was capable of doing such a thing. He displayed a different personality around our friends and pretended that he was the perfect husband, father, son, and person. He thought he didn't make mistakes. He often said, "I made my first mistake today."

Chris acted as if he was too much of a gentleman to hit his wife, and he didn't believe that any man should mistreat a woman or his family. He didn't have to have a reason to hit me; it could have been that he didn't like the way I looked, or maybe I said something he didn't like—whatever he felt like at the time, that's what he did. He was an explosive man. He made me feel like I didn't have a brain to think with and that I never did anything that was up to his standards.

Before Nicole left, we went shopping for groceries. As we were putting the groceries away, Chris came into the kitchen, and he looked at the checkbook to see how much money I spent. He looked at me and said, "You spent too much money!"

Nicole said, "Okay, dad, we can take the popcorn, salsa, chips and some of the other things that we don't need back."

"Oh no," Chris said, "Where do you think you are going with those things? That's alright!"

One day, we were sitting in the great room, and Chris said to me, "The reason I don't take you anywhere is because you don't know how to talk to people, and you have no conversation." He told me that to be in a relationship, you have to be friends, and we were not friends. I was hurt because I had been married to this nerd for thirty years, and now I was not his friend. I taught school, and I was in charge of the computer workshops for the teachers at school, and Chris thought I didn't know how to talk with people. This was Chris's opinion of me—the mother of his kids.

Chris didn't hit me again, but he sure whipped me with the verbal and mental abuse, which was just as bad or worse.

Chris started receiving alumni information from his college about homecomings and decided that we should go. The home-comings were always in October. Also, Brice had gotten invitations to attend a few college football games on Saturday, and we started going to those. Chris was having a ball going to the college games, especially because he didn't have to pay for tickets. Brice was invited to West Point, A&T, Winston Salem State, and Wake Forest games, and we did go to Colorado to an Air Force Academy football game.

Each year, we went to Chris's alma mater's homecoming, and we invited friends to meet us there. Once, we rode with a friend and his family. We always had a great time, and Chris was always nice around his friends.

THE EMPTY NEST 1989

Brice graduated from high school and enrolled in college. After he left, I began to understand what the empty nest syndrome was all about. When Nicole left, Brice was still home so that emptiness wasn't there.

One might say, "But you have Chris." I never had Chris; he was his own family. He often said, "I will be glad when the kids leave, so I won't have to do for them anymore."

My reply was, "What an awful thing to say. Suppose your mother and father had felt that way about you, where would you be?" As parents, we will always be there until that last breath is taken. You never stop being a parent. We will become old one day, and we hope they will be around.

With just the two of us, Chris spent a lot of time in Dillon helping his mother with her rental property. Additionally, Chris had bought a house that was across the street from his mom and rented it out. Mrs. Nora was collecting the rent for Chris.

My friend Marla, whom I graduated with from Fayetteville State, had gotten a job in a town nearby and wanted to stay with us until she could get settled. We told her she could; she was like family. She commuted to work everyday. She was a lot of fun, and I had someone to talk to.

When I was in private high school, I always wanted to pledge a sorority. Now that I had graduated from college, I had the opportunity to pledge a graduate chapter. I knew Nicole and a few of my friends wanted to as well. One friend lived in South Carolina, but she was willing to come here to pledge. This was the first time the sorority had a line in a very long time.

My friend in South Carolina found out that they had a line there, but Nicole and I pledged. After we completed the process, and Nicole and I went over. I was proud because once again I completed another goal that was important to me.

Chris and I started visiting his mother and Mr. Stiles more often, and he was still helping with her personal things. One Saturday that we were there, Chris noticed that Mrs. Nora wasn't keeping up with her bills and she was having trouble remembering what she was doing. The church secretary told him that Mrs. Nora had written some checks that had been returned. Chris tried to talk with her to understand what was wrong, and she told him everything was alright.

We noticed that Mrs. Nora was wearing the same clothes and layers of clothes. We began to notice a lot of things that she was doing that were out of character. Chris started asking close friends of hers if they noticed anything different about his mother, and they pointed out a few things to him that he should be concerned about.

In the meantime, Mrs. Nora and I were communicating, and that was good. One day when I was with her, I told her that I wanted to help her clean the house and make it pretty. She said that would be fine. Mrs. Nora was the grandmother of my children, and she was Chris's mother, and sometimes, someone needs to bite the bullet and make it right.

I started cleaning one room at a time. Mrs. Nora had a large house, and there were papers and books everywhere. We didn't spend the night; we went during the day and came back home late at night. After cleaning Mrs. Nora's and Mr. Stile's bedroom, I found clothes that belonged to Chris's father. I bagged the clothes, shoes, papers, and books and lots of stuff to throw out.

One weekend, Marla was off. She knew I was cleaning Mrs. Nora's house and agreed to go with us and help. We left that morning with Chris. When we arrived at Mrs. Nora's, we found that no one was home. Chris had a key, and we went in. Shortly after that, the doctors' office called and told Chris that Mrs. Nora was in the hospital, and he needed to come. At that time, we didn't know where Mr. Stiles was and had no way of contacting him. He was probably out gathering cardboard, which is what he did for extra money.

When we arrived at the hospital we found that Mrs. Nora seemed to be doing okay. Chris talked with the doctor's nurse, whose office was across the street from the hospital. They told him that his mother had been checked out and she was leaving when they noticed that she was wandering around in the parking lot. The nurse went out to check on her and realized that she didn't know where she was.

After talking with Mrs. Nora at the hospital, the doctor wanted to run some test and needed to admit her to the hospital. We made sure she was settled, Chris drove her car back to Dillon, and we followed him. As soon as we got to Mrs. Nora's, Mr. Stiles drove up and Chris immediately approached him with the situation at hand and demanded to know where he had been. Mr. Stiles was the kind of man who wouldn't argue, so he quietly stood there and took what Chris was saying to him. When you think about it, there was no way Mr. Stiles could have known what was going on with Mrs. Nora because cell phones weren't that popular; we didn't have one, either.

After Chris finished ranting at Mr. Stiles, I went outside to check on him; he was standing there crying. He said, "I didn't know Nora was sick." I know he was sincere because he really loved his wife.

We were getting ready to leave for Fayetteville, and Chris told Mr. Stiles to go to the hospital the next morning to check on his mother and that we would be back the next day.

They kept Mrs. Nora for a few days and Chris attitude changed towards me. He didn't want me to suggest anything or ask him anything about Mrs. Nora.

The doctor told Chris and Mr. Stiles that Mrs. Nora was in the early stages of Alzheimer's. He also told him that they would have to eventually place her in a nursing home. Chris talked with a family friend of Mrs. Nora's and she told him about someone that would be good to come and help Mr. Stiles with Mrs. Nora.

Chris called Mrs. Beaumont, who was a cousin of Mrs. Nora's, and she agreed to come in the mornings to help Mr. Stiles get Mrs. Nora dressed and her hair combed. Mr. Stiles would cook her breakfast.

Mrs. Beaumont went to the same church as Mrs. Nora and Mr. Stiles, and she started taking Mrs. Nora with her to visit church members and the sick and shut-in. When Chris found out that Mrs. Beaumont was taking his mother out of the house, he was furious and told her he didn't want her taking his mother out. He didn't want people to see his mother in the condition she was in. I thought this would be good for her to get out and visit her friends and people that she knew. This was part of the life she had before getting sick.

Chris said he didn't want Mrs. Beaumont to take her, and that was that. Mrs. Beaumont said Chris was also asking her to do things for him such as sewing hems in his casual pants that he wore to work. And, since he was in Dillon working on his mother's rental property, he wanted her to have dinner ready for them around five o'clock.

When I found out Chris gave Mrs. Beaumont a small amount of money a week, I was shocked. The stress he placed on her and the demands that she do things for him were too much, and she told him she wouldn't be able to help him anymore. I didn't blame her; there was enough money to pay for her services and be grateful to have someone that cared for his mother.

On Friday nights, I started asking Chris if he would be going to Dillon in the morning. He answered me with an, "I don't know." When Saturday morning came, he would be up and dressed telling me, "I will see you tonight." When I expressed surprise, since he hadn't known the night before if he would be going, his response was, "Well, I decided at the last minute." He would take his briefcase and tell me he would see me later.

The point was, he didn't want me to go. He always said, "You would be bored, and there isn't anything for you to do there, anyway." I didn't understand the logic; I had family and friends as well in Dillon—in fact, more than he did. I learned later that Chris was involved with his paramour, and I was in the way, so it was best if I stayed home.

He had a crew working with him to renovate his mother's rental houses so they would qualify for section eight housing, which is a government program that is based on the person's income. Chris spent a lot of hours supervising and getting acquainted with his housing inspector.

I suggested to Chris that he take his mom and Mrs. Stiles with us when we traveled. We knew that they enjoyed going. So we did this for almost six months; we took them to the Dillon Day celebrations and her family reunions.

Chris had gotten to the point that he didn't want to eat out with us, so he told me to take them out to eat and he would get a sandwich or something. He told me, "I have problems with Mom's eating habits; maybe you don't, but I do." I admit that it was difficult to watch someone as educated and intelligent as Mrs. Nora was—she had a Master's degree, taught school for forty years, was an elected city council person, and was very active in her church—brought to the level of almost being a child. I guess it was hard for him to accept, but we have to deal with it and get over it. It could just as easily be you in that situation.

We had a dear friend, Jennifer, who was in the military and stationed in Iowa. Chris thought this would be a good time to go out there for vacation. He started making plans and getting airline reservations to Chicago for three.

Chris's intention was to take his mother with us to Iowa. He knew Mr. Stiles was afraid to fly, and perhaps if he could get his mother away from him long enough, she wouldn't miss him and he could end that marriage. He didn't like Mr. Stiles and didn't think he was the right person for his mother.

Chris thought that Mrs. Nora's financial problems were because Mr. Stiles was spending her money. They were husband and wife, and she could do whatever she wanted to do with her money. They not only loved each other, they adored each other.

While we were gone to Iowa, Chris bought interior paint for Mr. Stiles to paint their living room. Mrs. Nora seemed to be okay for awhile; she didn't ask for Mr. Stiles too often—at least not until we arrived in Chicago and met Jennifer. She rented a car and made reservations for us in the Courtyard by Marriot in Chicago, and she also set up a bus tour for us.

Jennifer reserved adjoining rooms, which made it easier for me to help Mrs. Nora get cleaned up and dressed. Chris did nothing to help with his mother. When we went on the bus tour, he sat on the other side of the bus, and when we walked down the street, he walked behind us. In spite of his ways, we enjoyed ourselves and drove on to Iowa.

Mrs. Nora started asking for Mr. Stiles, and she was upset because she told Chris, "I need to go home to get my husband because some woman might take him." Jennifer and I reassured her that all was well. We called Mr. Stiles so she could talk with him, and that made things better for her.

While we were in Iowa, we decided to drive to Kansas to visit with Mrs. Harris, who was our neighbor in Fayetteville. She was like a mother to both of us, and she was like a sister to Mrs. Nora. We visited with her and spent the night in a hotel in Kansas. We really enjoyed seeing her.

We had a wonderful trip and returned to Fayetteville and took Mrs. Nora home to her husband. Chris admitted that he was wrong to try and separate them because he realized how much they meant to each other.

The next morning, I received a call from a local junior high school principal, and they wanted me to come for an interview.

Chris asked, "Are you sure you want a full time permanent job?"

"Yes," I told him, "this would be the first time I would actually have a contract teaching job in my field."

The interview went well; I was offered the job and started the next week. Chris seemed happy for me, but who knows? I completed and signed all the necessary papers, and I was hired as the business teacher for ninth grade; this is something I had always wanted to do.

Things were going well, until I found out from a friend of mine that Chris had approached her; I knew she wasn't lying because of the things he had said and what he had done. I knew she was telling the truth, because I had heard it before. I never said anything to him about it, but she told me that she felt that I should know.

I continued to deal with his infidelity and looked the other way. My job was going well, and I was happy with the school and my co-workers. The only time I would have a problem with working full time was when Chris's job required him to travel, and I wasn't used to staying home by myself. Marla, the young lady who was staying with us, had moved closer to her job.

So this was an adjustment for me, but I did okay. What Chris started doing was asking Mr. Stiles to bring his mother up here so they could stay with me and I could help him with her.

Just before I started my new job, I was cleaning Mrs. Nora's house. I thought it would be a good thing to give the house a thorough cleaning for her because she always had someone visiting her, and I knew she could not do this anymore.

It took me a good year to clean everything—hauling clothes, washing clothes, going though papers, washing walls, installing blinds in every room with the help of his stepfather, and hanging curtains. You name it, and I did it, even after I started working. I did this on the weekends. Little did I know that while I was doing all of this, Chris was having fun with his paramour. What she didn't know was that while he was cheating with her on me, he was also cheating on her with someone in Fayetteville, a friend of mine.

For some reason, Chris had mellowed out a little bit, but then he became very nasty and meaner than ever towards me. There were days he would not talk to me at all. In other words, the man was downright rude and obnoxious. I really didn't like him at all.

During our spring break, Chris suggested we go on a cruise to the Bahamas. This was our first cruise, so we made the reservations and drove to Florida. We spent the night, and the next morning, we boarded the cruise ship, Fantasy.

His attitude was good, and he was pleasant until we got on the ship. Chris's idea of having fun was to sleep. Therefore, I decided to leave him in the cabin. I found my way around and enjoyed the activities on the ship.

We did a four-day cruise, and I was glad it was over. On our way back to the Carolinas, Chris's attitude became abusive. He'd ask, "What are you doing that for?" Or, he'd demand, "Why did you say that?" Finally, he just stopped talking to me and gave me the silent treatment for about a week.

When he was ready to talk, he was the happy-go-lucky Chris. He didn't realize that maybe I was still trying to understand what was going on. After thirty years—it was our thirtieth anniversary—you think you know a person.

When I got home from work one evening, Chris said to me, "I need you to go somewhere with me." He took me to a jewelry store to find out if I liked a pearl ring he had picked out for me; it was beautiful and unique. He said the pearl symbolized thirty years of marriage. He had me try the ring on, and it had to be sized, but he wanted to buy it for me, and he did. Chris was the kind of person who wanted to be sure that I would let everyone know that he bought this ring for me for our thirtieth anniversary. When someone ignores you for a week, how can you get excited about a ring—or anything else for that matter? I was appreciative but not happy. Plus, he gave me thirty beautiful yellow roses; he knew they were my favorites.

In addition, Chris was building low-income rental property in Dillon. He applied for loans and, like clockwork, they came through. He always asked different friends of ours in Dillon, "Did she tell you about her new apartment building?"

I did not get excited about what Chris was doing; one minute, I was part of what he was doing, and the next minute, he would tell me he didn't want me to have anything to do with the projects and that he was a one-man show and that he did this all by himself.

Chris told me one time when we were sitting in the great room having a discussion that in order to have a relationship, you had to be friends. I thought that a relationship—marriage—was a commitment, and it had taken him thirty years to find out that he did not think I was his friend. Even after Chris had just spent money on a cruise, bought a ring to celebrate an anniversary, and had given me thirty yellow roses, he still thought that we did not have a relationship because we were not friends.

Chris's parents were coming to Fayetteville more often. Mrs. Nora's Alzheimer's was progressing, and her eating habits were still not good. She was not able to bathe herself, and she could not remember to go to the bathroom. Chris demanded that Mr. Stiles, and, of course, me take care of his mother's needs. I cared about the two of them and enjoyed being with them because they were fun, and they needed help; so I did what I could.

They started coming up on Friday evenings, and they stayed until Sundays and then went home to Dillon. When Chris went out of town, they came up and stayed until he returned. Eventually, on Fridays after I got of work, I began to drive them to Dillon and stay with them for the weekend so that they could go to church and visit with friends.

Chris and I cleaned his sister, Angela's room. We removed the carpet and the furniture, as well as the curtains, and we replaced everything, even putting up new blinds. We bought mattresses and put up a ceiling fan. The room was nice and comfortable. I even scrubbed the bathroom and put up blinds and curtains in there.

After getting Angela's room redone, we started spending the weekends in Dillon with his family. This was done so Mr. Stiles and Mrs. Nora could spend some time in their house.

Chris didn't want Mrs. Nora to go to church because he didn't want people to know that she was not herself anymore. She started doing other things that were out of character for her. She liked to ride and always wanted to get in the car. One time, she used a knife trying to unlock a deadbolt so she could get out. These things were embarrassing to Chris. She would often get up in the middle of the night and wander around.

He didn't want to go out with us to dinner anymore—as I mentioned before, Chris told me to take them to eat, and I did—she needed someone to help her and care for her, and Mr. Stiles couldn't do it all. Chris did very little to help with his mother. When I put her in the tub to give her a bath, I needed help getting her out. When I asked Chris to help me, he refused. Maybe he didn't want to see his mother nude, I don't know. I covered her with a bathrobe, thinking that would help. He finally agreed to help me.

One holiday, the kids were home and Chris decided to leave the house. We were not sure where he went. But Mrs. Nora and Mr. Stiles were visiting, and she was upstairs with him. She lost control of her bowels, and we all had to pitch in and help get her and the room cleaned up. We had to put the soiled mattresses in the garage until we could dispose of them.

When Chris came back and saw the mattresses in the garage, he immediately asked, "Why are the mattresses in the garage?" After receiving a brief explanation, he demanded, "When is someone going to clean them?" I told him this was not going to happen because they were ruined. After about a week or two, I came home from work and the mattresses were finally thrown away.

In April of 1997, I got a call from my eldest brother telling me that our mother had passed away. This was on a Friday evening. I called my kids, and they came home that Saturday morning so we could go home to see my family.

We left for Society Hill, and on the way, Chris said, "I guess we need to grill some possum!"

I said, "Are you making fun of my family?" He was cocky and a smart mouth. Nicole told him he shouldn't say things like that.

We got there and talked with my family and visited for awhile. My kids were not used to seeing the body lie in state in the house, which is what they always did.

The funeral was the next day. I told Chris he did not have to go back if he was uncomfortable with my family and wanted to make fun of them. He ignored me, of course. Nicole, Chris, and I left that morning and went back for the funeral. Brice needed to spend time with his study group, so he didn't go back with us.

Chris did not care if he offended someone; all he was concerned about was who the Jaguar that was parked in front of my mama's house and to whom it belonged. He thought it belonged to the funeral director, so he asked the young man who was driving it who the owner was. Lee, my cousin, told him the car belonged to his grandfather, my uncle.

That threw him for a loop; these people, he thought, could not own anything like that. All he saw was poverty and hillbillies. Because they didn't live in a four-bedroom, brick home and drive luxury cars and have a college education doesn't mean they don't have anything.

When we were getting ready to leave, Chris invited my family to come for a visit. He told them, "I have a big deck out back, and I'll grill some possum!"

"That's fine," my uncle said, "you can grill all the possum you want to, but we don't eat it!" I was too out-done; my family was always good to him, and, as far as they were concerned, he was family.

When we returned to Fayetteville, a friend of Chris's called and asked how I was doing. I said, "I'm doing better." He wanted to know if I had been sick, and I told him no, that my mother had passed. I thought Chris had told him. I learned that Chris didn't tell anyone; he was too concerned that they would want to go to the funeral and then he would have to explain who my family was and that he married into a white family. He wasn't going to put himself in that position.

After the comments that Chris made to my family about the possum, I realized he was a disturbed person. My family treated him with respect and love when we visited with them.

Chris wanted me to sign power of attorney over to him because he wanted to sell a rental house we owned. He thought I would back out, and he wouldn't be able to sell the property because we had joint ownership. I was not going to give him power of attorney so he could sign my name whenever he felt like it. I guess he thought I was completely stupid.

As time went on, I continued to bring his parents up to our home and then take them back to Dillon on the weekends. I had almost finished cleaning the house, with only a few more rooms to go. There were several people in Dillon who told me I was crazy for cleaning that house because of the way Mrs. Nora had treated me in the past. I told them that sometimes we have to do things out of love.

One holiday, Chris brought his parents to Fayetteville. He and the woman who was caring for Mrs. Nora did not pack enough clothes for her visit. Nicole and I went to Kmart and bought maybe two outfits for her. Later that evening, Chris went into one of his moods, and he was not talking to any of us. When I asked what was wrong, he told me that he did not appreciate me buying clothes for his mother. Because of this, he did not talk to me for least two weeks.

Chris went to Dillon and stayed for a few days while he helped someone work on another rental house that belonged to his mother. That was fine, but he did not tell me he was going to be gone. He just left; this was his way of punishing me.

My birthday was shortly after the Easter holiday. Chris was not talking to me and had not talked to me for a week or more; then he decided to send flowers to the school for me. He had his friend send flowers to me as well. He even called the school to find out if I had gotten them. My principal and co-workers thought that was the sweetest thing and what a loving, wonderful husband I had. This was Chris's way of showing others that he was a great person.

Chris came home that evening, and he was his usual self, grinning and talking to me as though he never stopped. He was friendly and wanted to know how I liked my flowers and what did my co-workers have to say about them. He also asked where I wanted to go for dinner. I wondered if he had a split personality or if he was narcissistic.

I went to Dillon with his family that Friday after work and Chris said, "I'll be there later, after I get off." He told me before I started taking them on the weekends that he did not want to go to Dillon, which was fine because he was someone I did not want to be around anyway.

Taking them to Dillon on the weekends, gave Mr. Stiles a chance to go to church, visit with friends, and just be in their house. When he realized that I was going to take them every weekend to Dillon, he said, "I might as well go with you, because there's no need to stay in Fayetteville by myself."

Chris had a meeting in Columbia, South Carolina, with the housing authority during the week of my birthday, and he told me if I wanted to go with him, I needed to be ready by the time he arrived in Dillon. I told him that I did not want to go, and he could go ahead. I did not like the tone in his voice. He was telling me, not asking me. I found out later why he was always glad I did not go. These meetings took place every year at the same time, which was in April and on my birthday.

When he came back from Columbia, we were still in Dillon, and this was the first time he did not get a gift for my birthday. I told him I needed a watch, so we drove to Sam's in Florence— not to buy a watch but to purchase a refrigerator from Circuit City for his rental property. Chris reluctantly agreed to buy the watch.

Chris's attitude with a couple of the employees at Circuit City was downright rude. He was like a time bomb waiting to go off. The people thought he was ready to pick up the refrigerator that they were getting ready to put it on the truck. He rudely said, "I don't want to pick up the refrigerator, I want to know if the ice maker is in there!"

The guys told him, "Everything is cool!" He didn't like them using slang with him; he said it was ghetto. When he was ready to pick up the refrigerator, the guy rolled it to the bed of the truck, and because of his attitude before, they didn't offer any more help than they were supposed to.

When we got in the truck and started back to Dillon, I used the word, "cool," not intentionally, and I was reprimanded; he told me that I sound like the people at the store: ghetto. Poor Chris does not understand.

I knew something was going on with Chris, and I knew that a woman was involved. There were too many trips to Columbia,

Dillon, and Florence, and his behavior was self righteous; he was so sure of himself.

One of those trips to Florence earned him a broken window on the passenger side of the pick-up truck he drove. He had to cover the window with plastic because he didn't have time to have it repaired. He told me someone tried to break in the truck while he was staying at a motel while on company business. Of course, no one took anything, and his vehicle was the only one broken into. To top that off, he wasn't upset about it.

Another time, Chris was in Columbia, South Carolina, and he picked up a refrigerator and a stove that belonged to a female friend who looked up to him as a big brother. He met her at the housing authority, and she told him he could have them so he could put them in the rental property.

While staying at the hotel in Columbia, he said he ran over some glass and cut his tire; luckily, his friend Monty was there, and he was able to get the tire repaired. Once again, Chris was not upset.

In response to all of these incidents, I say, woman scorned. I remember our son, Brice, asked his dad, "How many times can you apply for loans?" Chris answered that he could apply as many times as he wanted to. He said he was a one-man show when it came to the low-income housing, and he was successful in getting what he wanted. Chris had told me earlier, however, that they told him he could not apply anymore. That did not stop him from applying and getting more loans approved. He even told me that they were surprised that he was still being approved for loans.

At that time, I did not know that Chris had an inside interest. I found out that the trips to Dillon to meet with the housing inspector were also to meet with the woman with whom he was having an affair. She was promoted from housing inspector to the housing authority in the office where the loans were processed.

This is why Chris was treating me as if I were dirt; he was having another affair. Because of who she was and what she did, she was Chris's ticket to success and wealth. Approval of the loans happened every time he put in for one. I do not think Chris had a problem getting his loans approved. He told me it was easy to get the loans.

Chris had become so powerful financially that he decided to take his paramour to New Orleans for a four-day trip. I understand why he did not want me to have anything to do with what he was doing with the low-income housing. He and his paramour had everything under control; I was only in the way. However, he did not know how to remove me from his life, as long as I did not know he was actually playing both of us. In order to have his cake and eat it too, he had to use both of his women.

What tripped him up was having the itinerary sent to his house. His private life was soon to be revealed. He kept telling me that the company was building a plant in Louisiana, and he had to go help with the interviewing of new employees. I thought that would be great, because my sorority was having their convention in Louisiana, and I could go. I had never been to a sorority convention before, and it would be great to go to New Orleans. Not only that, but, school would be out for the summer; this was getting better by the minute.

THE ITINERARY COMETH
MAY 1998

I came home from work that evening; I think it was on a Thursday. I took the mail out of the mailbox, opened the garage door, parked the car, removed my school bag, and picked up the mail and my purse and went inside the house. As I entered the house, I usually put the mail on the counter in the kitchen; but this time, I took the mail and went into the great room and sat down.

I turned the television on, and then I started going through the mail. I put his mail on the sofa and started opening my mail. Then, I saw this envelope that had a return address from a travel agency in Charlotte, North Carolina, addressed to Chris. I looked at it and put it down; I didn't open his mail, not because he told me not to, I just didn't. For some reason, however, this was different. I picked it up, looked at it, and this time I opened it. It was an itinerary from a travel agency in Charlotte, North Carolina. I was getting excited because it read, "Chris Rushmore, destination New Orleans," and the date was June eleventh through the fourteenth, leaving from Charlotte airport.

I began to get a little excited because now I could make my plans to meet Chris in New Orleans for the convention since I had the dates and everything. Then something told me to reread the itinerary, so I started to read over the paper again. This time, I realized that I had overlooked the female companion who was traveling with Chris. I wondered who she was and thought that maybe she worked for the company and they were traveling together. As I read on, I noticed they were in the same hotel and going on a bus tour. I looked at the name, and a light bulb went off in my head. I realized that this man had arranged a trip to New Orleans with his paramour and had the gall to have the itinerary sent to his house. This had nothing to do with company business.

I decided to find out who the paramour was, so I called information in Columbia, South Carolina (just a hunch) and asked for the phone number for this person. I was told that this was an unlisted number. Good enough; I knew she existed and where she was.

I needed to be cool when Chris got home, because I didn't need to blow it. I put the letter back in the envelope and put it in my school bag. He had a habit of going in my purse for the checkbook, so he could check to see how much money I had spent, if any, that day. When he came in about five thirty, I was still in the great room, watching television. I wanted to tell him everything about the itinerary and that I knew about his paramour, but I knew there was a time for everything, and this was not the time.

He came in and said, "Hello, how was your day?"

I wanted to say, "Very interesting and that I gained a lot of information on you and your paramour!" But I didn't; I told him that I had a great day. He asked if I was ready to eat and said that if so, we could go to the diner and have dinner. I agreed.

We didn't talk too much on the way to the diner; I wanted to slap this man silly and put a strong hold on him, but I still had to play it cool. When we get to the diner and ordered our food, Chris copped an attitude. He didn't have to have a reason to get an attitude, but I was already angry. Then it came to me, how dare this man get an attitude with me in a public place or anywhere, when I knew that he has a paramour? I told him, "Look, I will not sit here and have you treat me this way!" I left the food and walked out. He paid for the food and followed me outside to the car.

"What is wrong with you?" he asked. I didn't say anything. I was quiet, and when we got home, I changed clothes and sat in the great room and watched television.

He went upstairs, which is what he always did anyway. He sat in the room where the computer was. When he came downstairs, I asked him if he had a tenant with the last name Washington. He replied that maybe he did. I sat up a little while longer, and then I went to bed. He didn't stay up too long before he came in the room and watched the news and went to bed.

The next morning, I said to Chris, "By the way, you got a call from a travel agency in Charlotte, and the man wanted to verify some information about your trip to Louisiana for the company. He stated that you have a traveling companion."

He said, "Oh no! That isn't right; I'll take care of it."

The next evening when we were at home, I began to tell Chris that since he was going to Louisiana, and we were having our convention and school would be out, I was thinking of joining him there. He told me that I would be bored because there would only be men. I told him I was going to attend the convention for my sorority while he was working. He told me to do what I wanted. I didn't bother him anymore that night.

That Saturday morning, we ate breakfast, sat and read the paper, and made small talk; then Chris went upstairs. This was Memorial Day weekend. After awhile, I decided to go up there to talk to him. When I went into the room where he was, he started telling me that he wanted to be alone so he could do what he wanted to do. The tears were falling and the nose was running, so I handed him some tissue. Then, I found myself almost pleading with him to let me help him. The look in his eyes told me to get out of there, and he began pounding on the table with his fist. I knew then that I needed to get out of there and quick.

I thought about the loans to build his low-income housing, how it had gotten easier to get the loans, all the rental property he had accumulated, and the kickbacks he had received from the loans, as well as the trips he made to Columbia, and Florence, and who knows where else. Chris all but put that woman at my dinner table.

I went downstairs and decided that the best thing for me to do was to get out there. I left and drove to Dillon. I was angry and hurt, knowing that this man had the nerve to destroy a family and a marriage of thirty-two years for money and a younger woman who could converse with him about the things he wanted to hear. I felt like a used car that had been traded in for a newer model.

After arriving in Dillon, I told Mr. Stiles and Mrs. Nora what Chris had done. Of course, Mrs. Nora did not understand what I was talking about, because if she had, Chris would not have made the move he did.

Chris and I talked over the phone during the weekend because he decided to stay in Fayetteville. That Monday evening, he finally came to Dillon.

I was not at the house when he got there, but when I arrived, everyone had gone to bed. Chris was in the bedroom with the door closed. When he realized I was in the house, I heard him go to the bathroom. I was lying on the couch in the den when he went back to the bedroom. I heard him lock the door; he was actually locking me out of the room, he thought.

I guess that meant not to bother him. I did not intend to sleep on that sofa in the den or anywhere else, not with my back problems. I decided it was time to take a stand, and I did. I went to the bedroom to open the door. I asked Chris, "Did you know that I can open the door by force, or you can open the door!" He responded that he needed to get some sleep. My response was, "Okay, but you were in Fayetteville for the weekend by yourself, and therefore, you should have gotten all the sleep you needed. If not, too bad; so open the door, for the last time!"

The door opened, and the first thing I noticed was that he had removed his wedding band. I knew then the marriage was over. He had never removed his wedding band before. I felt as though he hit me with a ton of bricks. I was not expecting this.

I told him if he was so unhappy living with me, he needed to leave. That is when he told me he had moved out of the house and would be living in Dillon with his mother and Mr. Stiles. Then, he said, "I owe you for the thirty-two years you have given me, and I will take care of you." Chris said a whole lot of stuff; he made promises that would soon be broken, just like the ones he made thirty-two years ago, when he made those wedding vows.

I had no idea my marriage would end after all those years. We stayed up the remainder of the morning, because I did not intend to let this man go to sleep. It just seemed like the thing to do.

I asked him how long it would take him to get the rest of his clothes out of the house. He said, "I don't know, I have a job in Fayetteville."

My adopted dad had surgery scheduled that morning at seven o'clock. Chris wanted to go and give him moral support because he said he had so much respect for him.

While at the hospital, he was trying to be cordial, and be the man everyone thought he was. He had the nerve to tell me that I needed to eat (I was diabetic). Therefore, for some reason, I met him at Hardees. I ordered my food and paid for it. He said, "I would have paid for your food." I didn't want him to do anything for me.

We actually sat down at the same table, and of course, he was being Chris, the charmer, behaving as though nothing had happened. I sat there, looked at him, and knew that I could not deal with him. I left and went to Mrs. Nora's house for a minute and then back to the hospital. After lunch, Chris popped in the door and said to me, "You need to eat lunch."

I asked him, "Why do you care?"

I left and packed my clothes and drove back to Fayetteville because I had to get ready for work the next day. This was Memorial Day weekend, and what a memorial Chris set up. The next day, his parents came up and brought my adopted dad from the hospital. I was at work when Chris came to the house, packed what clothes he wanted, and left. He left his parents at my house and went to Dillon; that was the last time he stayed in my house.

I talked with Chris later that evening, and I told him since he had moved out and would be going on his trip with his paramour, it would be alright for me to start dating. He told me that was fine as long as he didn't see me with them.

THE PRIVATE DETECTIVE AND NEW ORLEANS JUNE 1998

When I realized Chris actually moved his clothes out of the house, I knew then it was time for me to talk with an attorney.

I talked with a friend of mine, and she helped me find a private detective, whom I hired to accompany Chris and his paramour to New Orleans.

I needed proof of the affair to give to my attorney. She began filing court orders that would put a freeze on all assets, and he would not be able to turn of the utilities. I had a restraining order that kept him from coming to the house when he felt like it, in case Chris wanted to retaliate.

He came by the house one evening before I retained an attorney and gave me a check for three hundred dollars; he said that he was going to give me one blank check to use if I needed anything, with the stipulation that I write that check for a certain amount of money and consult him first. Even if I had thought to clean out the account, Chris would have a certain amount in there—no more, no less.

Chris did not want me to keep the checkbook; he was willing to give me an allowance until he could decide how much to give me each month based on the thirty-two years I had given him. He knew he would have complete control over his finances and me if I had accepted what he was proposing. I gave him the checkbook and his blank check. That blank check would have only been worth what he wanted it to be. These are reasons why I retained a lawyer and hired a private detective. I needed legal advice and proof to complete what Chris had started. He was furious with me because I had papers served on him, and he asked me not to serve them on his job. Chris did not think I was going to do what I did; he thought I would be satisfied with what he was going to do for me.

Arrangements had been made to meet with the detective. He told me what to bring, such as the copy of the itinerary, a photo of Chris, and few other things; then I had to sign a contract.

With the information I had given the detective, it would be easy to spot Chris at the airport. The detective said he would call my friend and let her know that Chris and his paramour were on the plane. Of course, my friend received the call, and they were at the airport waiting to board the plane.

The detective recognized Chris from the photograph I had given him. He started videotaping Chris and his paramour at the airport. They had to catch a later flight from Charlotte to Dallas, because their flight had been delayed. After arriving in Dallas, they had to stay overnight because of a flight that was cancelled to New Orleans.

After arriving in New Orleans, Chris and his paramour checked into room 244 at the Prytania Hotel. Chris decided to go to the front desk to purchase tickets to a jazz show; the private detective thought it would be a good idea to meet him and let him know who he was.

He introduced himself and started a conversation about the trip. He said that he had seen him at the airport and now again at the hotel. He told him his name, and, of course, Chris introduced himself. Rick told him he was a private detective and that he was hired by his wife to follow him and his paramour to New Orleans.

Once again, Chris was out done. The detective, Rick, said that Chris immediately left the lobby and went back to their room and placed a do not disturb sign on the door. I guess he forget to get the tickets to the jazz show.

I received a call that Chris had gotten on the plane; a few weeks later, I received a copy of the video and some other documentation I needed to give to the attorney.

Chris thought I did not have it in me; I didn't think I did either. I was proud of myself because I finally had the nerve to take control of my life; I had had enough.

FILING FOR MY FREEDOM AND A FULL PARDON

So now Chris could have all the time he needed to be alone and spend with his paramour.

Mr. Stiles called me from Dillon and told me he needed help with Mrs. Nora. He said Chris was not helping him. They were used to staying up and watching television as long as they wanted, but now that Chris was there. He told them to turn the television off because the noise disturbed him, and he had to get up at five o'clock to drive to Fayetteville for work. This was their house; Chris had chosen to leave his.

Mr. Stiles asked if he could come to Fayetteville with Mrs. Nora and stay with me. He said he could not live with Chris. So I told him to come; I didn't know he was going to stay permanently.

Mr. Stiles brought his wife to my house and said he didn't want to take her back to Dillon. Mrs. Nora would stay wherever he did. She was happy as long as she was with him. I told him to be sure this was what he wanted to do, because he was leaving their home and their church. He said he would be alright as long as he was away from Chris. He could not understand why Chris didn't like him.

Chris did not ask about his mother until some of their friends started asking how she was doing, and he really did not know. I think he was embarrassed because he was not keeping in touch with her.

One morning, Chris called me and said that Mr. Stiles needed to bring his mother to Dillon because that was their home and he wanted his mother there. I told him he needed to talk with Mr. Stiles, who was her husband and had the right to take his wife wherever he wanted to and stay as long as he wanted.

He didn't call Mr. Stiles to talk with him about bringing his mother back to Dillon; Chris was too busy having a good time as a single, free man enjoying his life with his paramour.

Court papers were served on Chris about the hearings, as well as the restraining order, which made him furious. He told me I had nerve to take out a restraining order against him, stating that he was a violent man. He didn't like the idea of having this recorded at the courthouse. Chris said, "It's commendable that I only hit you twice out the thirty-two years we were married!" I told him he did not hit me, he beat me. What is commendable about hitting a woman, anyway?

The man was driving from Dillon to Fayetteville everyday—that is an hour and a half one way. We make our choices even though we are senior citizens; there are times we do not realize that we have over-extended ourselves. He did this for about four years.

Chris had to go to Greensboro, North Carolina, on company business a couple of months after he moved out the house. Before he left, he changed the power from his name without telling me; therefore, my power was cut off. The company sent a man to my house and removed the meter. You know what that means: no power, no heat, no water, and no sewage.

After calling my attorney—this was in October—and telling her what happened, she contacted Chris's attorney, and before the power company closed that evening, my power was back on. This was not a pleasant situation because Chris's mother and stepfather were in the house with me. I could not have them sitting here in the cold.

A few weeks later, I decided that I needed to talk with Chris's paramour, so I called her office at the housing authority in South Carolina. I introduced myself and told her that my family and I forgave her for what she and Chris had done and that we would not be bothering her again. I was being the kind woman.

A little later, I decided that I needed to call her one more time because I forgot to tell her something, and I needed to have an emotional moment with her. This would make me feel better. I only needed to talk, no yelling, no cussing, just the facts. She was quiet and listened as I talked, and then she told me that Chris and I needed to work out our problems. She said, "I have nothing to do with the problems you're having." The thing is, Chris didn't tell me what the problems were except that he needed to have women on the side.

I told his parmour that she was part of the problem, she was in the mix. She was one of the reasons the man moved out, because he was caught taking her to New Orleans. She was on the video, on the plane, in the airport, and in the hotel room; her name was on the itinerary.

If I had not caught him with his paramour, Chris said himself that he would still be here. Chris would be here making everyone's life miserable.

I was even going to sue the paramour for alienation of affection. Under the advisement of another attorney, however, I dropped the case because she was not financially worth the effort.

I stated earlier that the man and the woman are to blame when a family is broken up; first, the outside woman knows whether the man is married and has a family. It did not matter if there were problems or confusion going on. Learn to say no and send the fool home. Why deal with someone else's leftovers?

She knew Chris was married; she knew where he worked and what his position was, as well as his educational background and what he owned and how many children he had. She knew because she had his financial background from the applications that he used to apply for the loans to build low-income housing. She knew everything about me, but I knew nothing about her. I am sure Chris talked a good game, but he didn't think he would get caught, and in the worse way.

In my opinion, with all the knowledge she had of my family, and being a woman with a Christian background, she should have just said, "No." She knew this was wrong from a spiritual standpoint. The man was married, but she was looking for a husband, and it did not matter whose husband he was. I know if a man or woman wants to leave a marriage, he or she will leave. I believe some, not all, will leave if they have a reason waiting outside the home to stroke their egos.

If you have been married for thirty-two years and become involved with a woman or man (for three years), one might ask what took you so long to leave, if you really wanted to be with that woman or man; does getting caught give you the reason to leave? Therefore, catching Chris in his affair was the worst for him. Chris had someone waiting to give him all that he thought he needed. You have to care for the grass, no matter where you are, to keep it green.

I spent five years of court drama with Chris deliberately not sending my alimony one Christmas, which caused me a hardship as far as being able to get my medicine. Chris has no compassion for others. Not only did I have scoliosis, I was diagnosed with diabetes in 1992. Years before he left, in fact, Chris was in the doctor's office with me agreeing and encouraging me to go on insulin to help regulate my blood sugar and assuring me that he would help me. He was well aware of my medical issues.

I applied for disability through Social Security, and I received the award the first time applying. This does not ordinarily happen. I am not saying that God wants us to be disabled, but sometimes, I believe He allows some things to happen in our lives. We had a court hearing shortly after I started receiving my disability. Chris and his attorney questioned my disability, and he was not happy because this would mean I would only be allowed to make up to a certain amount of money per month. Chris wanted to see proof as to why I received disability.

Chris said there was nothing wrong with me and that I was faking it so I could get more money out of him. A little medical history here: I had surgery on my upper spine because of bone spurs that could have caused paralysis. I was already having problems with my left arm being numb and cold, and I was having problems turning my head to the left. The surgery that I had on my spine took seven hours. The recuperation period was three months. I was injecting insulin twice a day for diabetes since 1994, and Chris was part of that decision. Chris was so supportive of me going on insulin. One morning, about three o'clock, I woke up because I didn't feel good. I decided to check my blood sugar to see if my level was okay. My level was twenty-seven. I started doing the necessary things to bring it back up. I was shaking and incoherent so I was having problems thinking. In the midst of this situation, I noticed Chris standing near the refrigerator. He said nothing. Did he know what to do to help me? Yes, he had gone to the diabetic classes with me; I gave him my diabetic book so he could read it and that would let him know what was going on with me.

I continued to check my blood sugar, and when I looked up to see where Chris was, he had left; he went back to bed. My caring husband was obviously not concerned; he did not ask me the next morning what happened or if I was okay.

I thanked God because He woke me up and was the one who gave me the strength to do what I needed to do to take care of myself. I remember a friend told me to eat food to bring my blood level up.

Because of my back problems, my orthopedic specialist gave us a prescription for an orthopedic mattress, which benefited Chris as well, and the insurance company paid for it.

As I said before, Chris's paramour worked at the housing authority as a housing inspector when Chris met her in 1995. Her inspections were not only of low-income section eight housing but of him as well. Shortly afterward, his paramour started working in the office where the loans were processed. Chris was not having a problem getting loans to build low-income housing. She was the key to part of his success. She was in a position to give him the guidance he needed to work through the application process to get the loans approved. I am not saying that she had the power to approve the loans but the know-how to get them approved.

She knew Chris was getting excess money from the loans after the contractors made their bids. He had two options in Dillon and started taking the option he knew that suited him and the contractor.

With some of the excess money, Chris paid the balance of the mortgage owed on this house before he left in May. I know Chris; he never would have paid for this house if he had made plans to leave his family.

We do not know at the present time what is best for us, but Chris's present wife had no idea what she had done for me. She made it possible for me to have a stress-free life.

I wanted to give the video of the New Orleans trip to the paramour's supervisor, but under advisement from my attorney, I did not because of the legal ramifications.

Remember, I told you I called Chris's paramour twice and talked with her each time. After I made the second call, she had an attorney contact my attorney with a letter stating that I was stalking and harassing and threatening her, and if I continued to do so, there would be legal action taken against me. I told my attorney I had an emotional moment and that after that second call to her, I had emotional satisfaction and I was through talking to her.

As far as stalking her was concerned, I did not intend to waste my time, gas, or energy following her around; that was for Chris to do. Besides that was not part of my character—she didn't know that, but Chris did.

The year of legal separation was up, and Chris filed for a divorce. Two weeks later, he married his paramour and moved her and her family to live with him in a different part of South Carolina.

The court at that time had awarded me with temporary alimony. I was to receive the rent from the house we previously lived in. I did not have the support money sent through the court, which is what I should have done, but I was not thinking. Instead, Chris wrote the check for the rent, and his wife wrote the check for the temporary alimony and the power bill as well as a check for medical benefits.

I was sensitive about her sending me a check; some of my acquaintances asked what difference it made, as long as I got it. That is true; however, they had done enough, and there was no need to rub it in my face.

In the meantime, Mrs. Nora's condition was getting worse, and she was not capable of making decisions for herself, but her husband could. Mr. Stiles and Mrs. Nora were still living with me.

Chris took control over Mrs. Nora's income, and he made the decision to send three hundred dollars a month to provide for her. He completely ignored the fact that Mr. Stiles was his mother's husband. Mr. Stiles had only his social security income, which he used to clothe, feed, and care for his wife. They loved each other, and Mrs. Nora did not want Mr. Stiles out of her sight.

The courts here in North Carolina ruled that Chris had no legal rights to his mom. Because Chris had control of Mrs. Nora's income and was not using it for her, he had to give all that up.

I wanted nothing to do with her money, but I agreed to help Mr. Stiles take care of her. The court appointed an attorney as guardian to take care of her finances, and, as her guardian, I agreed to help Mr. Stiles take care of her personal needs. The attorney was supposed to take care of her home and rental property she had in South Carolina, which his office did not do. Shortly after the court decision, Mr. Stiles and I continued to do what was best for Mrs. Nora.

We finally, under the advice of her doctor and the adult daycare givers, had to place her in a facility that provided assisted living, and Medicaid and Medicare took care of her expenses. She was doing well and missed her husband.

Mr. Stiles was tired, and he felt that Chris, being her son, should share in the care of his mother. Chris moved Mrs. Nora back to Dillon and placed her in a nursing facility. Mr. Stiles moved to Dillon so he could be close to this wife. He could not move back in the house he and his wife had lived in because Chris arranged to rent the house and disposed of the furniture.

Then, Chris decided to take Mr. Stiles to court for a hearing in Dillon to have him declared incompetent. Results were in Mr. Stiles' favor. You see, Mr. Stiles was living with his cousin down the street from the house he lived in with Mrs. Nora.

So the court made a ruling that Chris was to prepare the rental house across the street from the main house for Mr. Stiles; he was to install central heat and air and return what furniture Mr. Stiles wanted to that house.

Sometimes, when you try to dig a hole for one, you need to dig two. Mr. Stiles and Mrs. Nora had a car that they paid for each month. Mr. Stiles made the check out to Chris for the car each month. Chris's vindictiveness toward Mr. Stiles was unforgivable; he did not want him to have anything. Chris bought the car owned by Mr. Stiles and Mrs. Nora. He knew Mr. Stiles had no transportation, but he watched him walk wherever he had to go, including visiting his wife. Somehow, the title was in Mrs. Nora's name; therefore, that left Mr. Stiles out.

Chris bought the car and later gave it to his stepson. Chris knew Mr. Stiles needed transportation to get around in Dillon and to visit his wife, but he had no problem knowing that this man had to walk wherever he went and had to catch a ride or get a taxi to take him to see his wife. Mr. Stiles was a survivor; he was a kindhearted man, and he was the type of person who did not hurt anyone, did not speak a cross word, and always cared a lot about Chris. Mr. Stiles would have done anything for him. He even asked Chris to forgive him if he had done or said anything to hurt him. Chris told him he would not forgive him, and he would take it to his grave that he put his mother in a nursing home.

I believe God had a plan for those two. God knew Mrs. Nora would need someone to take care of her—someone who truly loved her and not her things. He was exactly the kind of man that God put in her life. They enjoyed each other; they had fun, laughed a lot, and made each other happy.

Many people thought she should have married an educated, professional man. Mr. Stiles did not have a college degree, and his profession was one that did not require a college degree, but he was a God-fearing man with a heart full of love. If more marriages were like theirs, there would be fewer divorces.

Chris moved Mrs. Nora back to the homestead, which was a blessing for Mr. Stiles because he did not have to worry about finding someone to take him to see her, all he had to do was walk across the street. Isn't God good? He gave Mr. Stiles favor.

Mrs. Nora lived about a year after moving her home, and Chris did not acknowledge Mr. Stiles. It was as though she had no husband; Chris made all the arrangements for his mother's funeral. Neither Mr. Stiles nor Mrs. Nora's grandchildren knew about the arrangements. They had to contact Chris to find out about the final arrangements.

Mr. Stiles, his son, and his daughter-in-law came the day before the funeral. They bought him a new suit and the accessories to match for the funeral, went to the florist, and purchased a flower. Everyone except Mr. Stiles rode in a limousine, including the grandchildren. Mr. Stiles walked to the church to his wife's funeral. When he arrived at the church, a cousin took him in with her. He was not in the family processional and did not take his rightful place in the church.

This was just the way Chris wanted it. I know what I am talking about; Chris disliked—I will not use the word hate; that is too harsh—him that much. Chris did not acknowledge Mr. Stiles at all.

Benjamin, Mr. Stile's son, put in for the benefits from Mrs. Nora for his father. Chris had already told the retirement personnel that Mrs. Nora didn't have a living spouse, and he changed the document that stated that Mr. Stiles was the official beneficiary on her state burial document. Mr. Stile's son was able to get everything straightened out, and Mr. Stiles was able to receive benefits from his wife, which he deserved.

He still visited with me, and, shortly afterward, his son moved him to South Carolina, where he lived. His health was failing some, and he needed to be in a secure place. Shortly after his stay in the health facility, Mr. Stiles passed away. Before he passed, Chris found out where Mr. Stiles was and went to the facility. He sent his wife inside to get Mr. Stiles to sign some papers, which would have caused him to relinquish his rights to any of Mrs. Nora's estate; fortunately, Chris's plan backfired. The wife was trying to leave because Mr. Stiles told her no, and the nurse called Benjamin to let him know what was going on. Just as Chris's wife was trying to get through, the automatic door closed and her skirt was caught; she was finally able to get free, and she immediately left the premises with Chris waiting in the car outside in the parking lot. The facility notified Mr. Stiles' son to let him know what was going on; but before he could get there, they were gone.

We were still in litigation, and Chris was trying to give me what he wanted me to have. I was tired and wanted to give in, but I knew I could not do that. When you have given someone thirty-two years of your life, you do not lie down and die. You have to stand up and fight for what rightfully belongs to you. I had to put on the whole armor of God because without Him, I couldn't make it. I was tired of the abuse mentally and physically, and it was my turn to play ball.

I had one of the best attorneys, and she was willing to fight for me. I knew God had not brought me this far to leave me. When you always put yourself last and put others first, which is what I did constantly, sooner or later, it becomes your turn.

I did not fight dirty, and I was not revengeful, although there were times that I wanted to be. I tried to be fair with my demands. However, I knew that what God had for me was for me. Chris did not think I was worthy or capable of using my brain; he always thought someone else did my thinking for me—not this time. Therefore, I stood firm and strong, and I told my attorney that

I trusted God and that I trusted her to make the right decisions for me. This is my future we were talking about.

I gave this man my youth and past; now it was time for him to be a man, and if it meant taking care of two women, so be it.

After we could not reach an agreement concerning the distribution of property, we had to meet with a mediator, which was almost an all-day affair. By this time, the company where Chris worked was going through a transition; they were closing. They did close their doors, and they terminated Chris's position and distributed his duties to other people within the plant. This meant that after thirty years in the Fayetteville area in industry, he was gone. Ordinarily, Chris would have been offered a job somewhere else, but not this time. There was an offer to buy the plant, and it was purchased by some other company, but Chris was not offered a job with this company, either.

It took five years to reach an agreement in the courts for the distribution of property. Chris was so intimidating that I had trouble sitting in the same room with him. I finally reached the confidence level where it did not make a difference. I was able to face that giant in my life, and it felt good.

We had to go into mediation in order to reach a decision to settle the distribution of property. This took several hours, but a decision was made. Chris was not satisfied because he felt that everything was his, and I did not deserve to have what he had worked for all by himself. We needed to either reach a decision, or the judge would have to make it for us. After we reached an agreement and signed the documents, just before I left, I reached across the table and extended my hand in thanks to Chris's attorney, and then to Chris, who turned his back to me and looked out the window.

I received half of the estate that we accumulated over the thirty-two years of marriage. We still had to go to an alimony hearing, which took place a few weeks later. I was given alimony for the rest of my life or Chris's life, whoever died first, or until I decided to get married. Why would I want to remarry? I was married to Chris for thirty-two years, which I consider to be a lifetime. I am not saying that it will never happen, but right now, no. I am too busy enjoying my life, and we have to take time and heal from broken relationships and not carry that baggage into a new one. As I said, I am enjoying my life, my children (the grown ones), and mostly my grandchildren, those little blessings.

I started going to counseling in 1998, and, after a few sessions, I realized this is something I should have done years before. If it had not been for counseling and God, I would not be writing my memoirs, and I would not have been able to face the giants I was dealing with—not just Chris.

Along with the relationship I had developed with God and learning to trust him—I mean really trust him—I have to give thanks to God during the bad times, hard times, and the good times. Thanking God and giving Him praise when things are going rough is awesome if you learn to focus on Jesus. He already knows where you are going. He knows where he brought you from, and He will let you take baby steps to get where you need to go. We do not realize that God carries you all the way. We just need to trust in him.

Put him first (seek ye first the kingdom of God and all his righteousness and the things will be added). Is it easy to do? Not really, because we make things hard.

Once we realize what God is asking us to do and commit ourselves and are obedient to His word, we can do all things through Christ, who strengthens us. The things we do for material gain are and can be dangerous in our lives if we focus on ourselves and not on the glory of God.

I hope that what I am writing will benefit someone else. The abuse from those you care about, whether it's physical or mental, and having to deal with society and the rules that you have to deal with can give you a lot of heartache in life. In a way, it should not make a difference because God knows who and what I am. However, the flesh side of me wants to know if I fit into the world that my sister and brothers live in.

When I think about it now, there was no integration until the sixties; so I wonder if I broke some racial barriers without being aware of it. I was a member of a black church, went to black schools, lived and socialized with blacks, dated black guys, joined a black sorority, became a member of the NAACP, married a black man, graduated from a black college, and lived as a black person from the age of seven to now. Is this what God had planned—for me to grow up and realize that we can be different and no one really notices anymore? Maybe my experience had to be told in order to help someone else who may be displaced in society.

That is what happens to many people like me seeking a place to belong. No one really noticed where I came from. I was totally aware of what was going on in my life, even as a child.

These things can have an impact on your future, depending on how you learn to handle what life throws at you. What happens to those of us who have the same-race parents and siblings, but one turns out to be different? I fit into the black culture with no problem. I do not know what living in the white world is about. I image it would be the same—the problems are the same, but because of how and where I was raised, I have difficulty feeling comfortable when I return for visits with my family. Believe me, it is different.

People who were so close to me during the first seven years of my life were my family—a family that loved me and had my best interest at heart enough to let me go. Those that I called family had my interest at heart only when it accommodated them. After that, I was an outsider, a commodity. I did not belong to anyone there, not even a cousin by blood; I was always the girl that Lennie and those had raised. I was soon forgotten, and maybe a faint memory in the minds of some.

So my destiny is to tell others that it is alright to be different, as long as you know that you are a child of God. Not only are we different but we are special. We have destinies and a purpose in life; I fulfilled mine with my children, and God blessed me with a girl and a boy. I am so proud of the way they have grown to become wonderful adults.

There are other children who have had an impact on my life; I call them my little brothers and sisters. They spent time with me for various reasons, and they were blessings to me. Oh, what joyous blessings they were; the memories they gave me and a piece of their growing up that will always be embedded in my heart. Some knew about my background and found it to be fascinating and did not love me any less. Some made no comments at all, and some had their theories about my background.

I have to believe that with all that went on in my life, meeting Chris Rushmore and marrying him was not by chance but part of my destiny. Had it not been for him being a part of my life, there would be no Brice or Nicole. I would not be in Fayetteville; I would not have met all the people that I have during the latter years and experienced the things that I did in my life. I would not be divorced, would not have gone to counseling that made me aware of who I am. I would not have gained the strength and knowledge to sit down and put all this history in writing so that maybe the whole world will be made aware that once again, it is alright to be different.

Thank you, God; I am somebody, and I am special. So thank you, God for planting the seed of Grace and Love in my life.

Thank you, Chris for helping me realize that life has many avenues. When you made the decision to move on, you relinquished the power that you used to stifle me. You are no longer an albatross in my life. Now, I have a full life of joy, happiness, and peace.

You may realize it now, but ten years ago you did not—life does not revolve around you, Chris. People have been making decisions for many years without you. Education was around when you were born, and everyone had the opportunity to accomplish the same goals you did and are successful.

It does not take a college degree and money to make a man—it helps, but it takes wisdom, love, and a relationship with God to be a whole and complete man.

AFTER THOUGHTS

Chris told me he owed me for the thirty-two years I had given him, and he would continue to take care of me. How do you pay a wife of thirty-two years for her life that she gave you? Including the jobs she had over those years: having children for you, being a teacher, a housekeeper, the cook (good or bad), yard maintenance, nursing, counseling, bedroom drama, entertainer, office assistance, dental assistant, window washer, car washer, daycare worker, and I am sure there are more professions that are included. When you add up the salaries of each one of those professions for the year, the government cannot pay a wife and mother what would be owed, so what makes Chris think he could?

I am trying to establish a relationship with my biological family, looking after my adopted father, who will soon be ninety-two years old and resides in a nursing facility here in Fayetteville. I also check on my godmother, who is ninety-three years of age and resides in a nursing facility in South Carolina. I have spent a few years writing, traveling, and strengthening my relationship with God and some old friends. I realized that we are all children of God, and it should not make a difference what color our skin is, because with God, He is no respecter of persons; we are all the same in His eyes.

Since slavery, we have been classed into races and taught to believe that one was superior to the other. When in reality, we are all the same. Now, times have changed, and some people do not know what their race is anymore and don't want to know. We have a multicolor culture, which was started during slavery not in this generation. Now it is legal, then it was not.

What we have now is a race of beautiful people of all colors, which one day will become the majority. What impact does this have on a child's mind, as they grow older? Sometimes, there can be an identity problem, and it can matter. I think it depends on where you live and the mindset of some people, how you are received, and the parents.

Instead of stating your race, it has become optional, or there is a space for "other." There should not be a space at all to distinguish among races. It should not make a difference, because we are female or male, we can work, we are human beings, and we are God's children. Class us as people. Stop the division and come together as the people of this country, this world.

As I conclude my thoughts, my memoir, there is a change taking place (2008). We have an African-American running for President of the United States of America; he happens to be the son of a white-born Kansas mother and a father who is from Kenya (Africa). Now, how do you class him? He says he is a human being; that is true. However, some of us feel the same way but still have identity problems. Since this is another time and era in this great country, it should not matter—he meets all of the qualifications required to run for such a powerful office, and, God willing, could win.

As a little girl born in the year 1943, in South Carolina. I was not given the opportunity to go to school because of the color of my skin and because my hair was not straight; I was not a blonde-haired, blued-eyed child. I was the third eldest child born to a white mother and white father. There were three other siblings born to the same parents, none of whom were blonde or blue eyed, but they were accepted.

Now the candidate running for office was raised by his grand-parents, who were white, but because of the time and era, it still did not seem to make a difference.

In the book of Ecclesiastes, scripture says, "There is a time and Season for all things." This is the candidate's time and season. My time and season was during segregation, and I still broke barriers that were not even thought about because of the circumstances and the way my life was played out.

This is the way it is supposed to be. Now is the time to open the book and release the chapters of the life of a little girl born to Eva Bryant Chapman and Edwin Chapman, who had the opportu-nity to see her little girl grow up in a culture that, at that time, was best for her. She was very proud.

Now she has been born again, but this time with God as her Father, who will raise her differently. He will bless me with unconditional love and everlasting life. Thank you, God! Thank you, Mama, for making a decision that had to be difficult—but you made it, and look at your daughter now.

No matter what I had to go through from a little girl to now, God had a plan for my life. The love I have for you, Mama, is beyond the reach of the world. You are my Star—the one that kept me going no matter what—and my guardian angel. I do not know if I could have done what you did.

Now that you know practically everything there is to know about me and my life, the time has come for me to enjoy the rest of that life with dignity, peace, and joy, accepting the difference and seeing the changes in this world.

I believe only in things that God puts before me, and I will be the person He wants me to be and more if He desires until He calls me home.

Thank God! Thank God! Thank God!

I LOVE YOU IVY AND DONDREI!!!!!

Made in the USA
Lexington, KY
05 October 2010